Advance Praise for *Mining the Soul*

In *Mining the Soul*, Robin Robertson skillfully describes the most profound aspects of the human psyche and how they can be accessed. His readers will gain new insights into the brain, dreaming, synchronicity, intuition, and Eastern thought and practices. If [people] put Robertson's suggestions to work, and follow the exercises he articulates, [their] lives may never be the same again.

—Stanley Krippner, Ph.D.
Co-author of *The Mythic Path*
co-editor of *Varieties of Anomalous Experience*

———◆◆◆———

In a secular era, bereft of spiritual resources, Robin Robertson recovers the wisdom of antiquity—that meaning is found from within the individual and tribal psyche. To facilitate access to this rich source, our ancestors developed divinatory methods at which the modern sensibility scoffs. But Robertson, weaving modern brain research with dream work, active imagination, the *I Ching*, chakra therapy, meditation, and other methods, recovers these apertures to informing vision and reconnection with our spiritual nature. Robertson is a great teacher, for he is able to assimilate complex research and uncommon concepts, distill them, and communicate them to the reader using clear prose, common sense, and simple eloquence. Such teachers are a gift to us all.

—James Hollis, Ph.D., Jungian Analyst
Author of *The Archtypal Imagination*

———◆◆◆———

Robin Robertson at his best—accessible, down-to-earth, and profound. A superb introduction to the life of the unconscious.

—Richard Smoley
Co-author *Hidden Wisdom:*
A Guide to the Western Inner Traditions

I am an unabashed fan of Robertson and was especially impressed by his book on Jungian Archetypes, an exploration of the relationships between Jung and Godel. *Mining the Soul* combines three levels of Robin's mastery, the lucid explanations of an authority on his subject, the survey of a great deal of relevant research and theory, and down to earth personal experience with dreams and the psyche that make the story more convincing and interesting. For those who keep putting off the resolution to start a dream diary, he convinces us to put it off no longer by showing both how it can be learned and how meaningful it is, although I myself am interested more for its intrinsic existential value in creating, rather than discovering, a personal destiny.

As a brain scientist and chaos theorist, I have vaguely speculated on the dynamical systems aspect that views dreaming as involving a change in couplings between brain systems, and was especially intrigued with Robertson updating us on how far this thinking has progressed.

—Frederick David Abraham
Author of *A Visual Introduction to
Dynamical Systems Theory for Psychology*

———◆•◆———

Robertson has given us a book of wonders; a delightful tour of the mind that itself opens up from the inside out. It will take its place beside Robert Johnson's *Inner Work* as a masterful guide to the mystery and the miracle of what it is to be human. Here, Robertson calls upon his extraordinary knowledge of Depth Psychology, computer technolgy, myth, and the brain, to weave the inside out story of our lives. Read and enjoy.

—Allan Combs
Author of *The Radiance of Being*

Robin Robertson is a traveler in two worlds, or what C. P. Snow called, the two cultures. In *Mining the Soul*, he once again demonstrates his expertise as a guide through these two worlds, and what's more, he clearly and powerfully demonstrates that the two worlds are actually one.

Robertson—psychologist, mathematician, magician—brings to bear the full range of his marvelous, eclectic knowledge of the inner world of Depth Psychology, and various arcane traditions, and the outer world of empirical science, creating a convincing synthesis of the two.

Having presented his thesis that we live our lives from the inside out, he shows that the inner world can best be entered by means of gateways and rituals, and then proceeds to guide us through the realms of dreams, synchronicity, meditation, chakra lore, and divination with particular attention given to the *I Ching*. He makes these gateways accessible to our understanding through a thorough and wide-ranging discussion of the most recent investigations in brain research.

As always, Dr. Robertson's lucid prose has the almost magical effect of rendering not only the opaque constructions of science and mathematics, such as those on the holographic universe and chaos theory, vividly clear, but also the seemingly mysterious propositions of divination and Jungian Active Imagination.

This book is breathtaking in its scope and truly inspiring in its goal, which I believe it succeeds in attaining; that nothing less than showing how the two worlds are one meaningful whole—of which our lives are a meaningful part.

—Richard Messer
Poet and author of *Murder in the Family: Poems*

The world of consciousness has its spokesman in Robin Robertson. He's becoming a "name brand" when it comes to explaining in fresh terms the important mysteries that lie within us. Use his book as a guide and you'll discover within yourself the buried treasure that already knows your real name!

"Know Thyself!" This well-known, but mostly ignored, prescription for enlightenment contains a closely guarded secret. Robin Robertson, whom we can count on to guide us into the realm of consciousness in a totally fresh manner, reveals the secret to us. Practice the exercises he suggests, and you'll discover an inner dynamo that creates the world in which you live.

—Henry Reed, Ph.D.
Dream pioneer and author of
Your Mind: Unlocking Your Hidden Power

------◆◆◆------

Dr. Robertson is a masterful teacher who weaves the threads of brain research, Jungian Psychology, mysticism, meditation, and magic in a way that entertains and informs. I found myself utterly intrigued with his unique insight into that pair of opposites: inner and outer. This fine book is for professionals who want a new and really good tool for their psychological tool kits, and for lay people who wish to learn how to penetrate the mysteries of the psyche. Robertson speaks with authority, clarity, humor, and depth. I'm planning to buy a dozen copies to give to friends who ask *me* to explain Active Imagination, Brain research, the Collective Unconscious, or the *I Ching*. Robin Robertson's *Mining the Soul* does it better.

—Gilda Franz
Co-editor, *Psychological Perspectives*

MINING THE
SOUL

On The Hudson
Jung
BOOK SERIES

The Jung on the Hudson Book Series was instituted by the New York Center for Jungian Studies in 1997. This ongoing series is designed to present books that will be of interest to individuals of all fields, as well as mental health professionals, who are interested in exploring the relevance of the psychology and ideas of C. G. Jung to their personal lives and professional activities.

For more information about this series and the New York Center for Jungian Studies contact: Aryeh Maidenbaum, Ph.D., New York Center for Jungian Studies, 41 Park Avenue, Suite 1D, New York, NY 10016, telephone (212) 689-8238, fax (212) 889-7634.

For more information about becoming part of this series contact: Betty Lundsted, Nicolas-Hays, P. O. Box 2039, York Beach, ME 03910-2039, telephone (207) 363-4393 ext. 12, email: nhi@weiserbooks.com.

From the Inside Out
MINING THE SOUL

ROBIN ROBERTSON

NICOLAS-HAYS, INC.
York Beach, Maine

First published in 2000 by
Nicolas-Hays, Inc.
P.O. Box 2039
York Beach, ME 03910-2039

Distributed to the trade by
SAMUEL WEISER, INC.
Box 612
York Beach, ME 03910
www.weiserbooks.com

Library of Congress-in-Publication Data

Robertson, Robin
    Mining the soul : from the inside out / Robin Robertson.
        p. cm. — (A Jung on the Hudson book)
    Includes bibliographical references and index.
    ISBN 0-89254-055-9 (pbk. : alk. paper)
    1. Spiritual life. I. Title. II. Jung on the Hudson book series.

BL624 .R622 2000
150.19'54 — dc21   00–033939

VG

Cover art copyright © 2000 Eveline Taylor
Cover design by Kathryn Sky-Peck

Typeset in 10/12 Book Antiqua

Printed in United States of America

07 06 05 04 03 02 01 00
8   7   6   5   4   3   2   1

The paper used in this publication meets the minimum requirements of the American National Standard for Information Sciences — Permanence of Paper for Printed Library Materials Z39.48-1992 (R1997).

To Monte Zerger—
for without your help and encouragement,
this book would not have come into being.

CONTENTS

ACKNOWLEDGMENTS

I would like to thank Monte Zerger for the considerable effect he has had on this book, which originally began out of a desire to find some project on which we could work together. During the research phase, we had extensive correspondence, for Monte is a cornucopia of ideas, especially those related to the strange and beautiful appearance of mathematics within the fabric of the world. He also supplied many astonishingly apt quotations from a variety of sources, only some of which appear in this book. As I began writing, however, I found that my idiosyncratic writing habits make it nearly impossible to collaborate with anyone. My books always come out of the unconscious, which I trust implicitly, but this means that every book evolves in directions impossible to predict in advance. Material often appears in the early chapters which would seem to be totally out of place, and which only gradually reveal their raison d'etre. Even after it became clear that this couldn't be a joint work, Monte continued to help me at every stage, enriching the book in many ways.

I'd also like to acknowledge Henry Reed's willingness to share his profound dream with readers, as well as allowing me to present a tiny look at his repertoire of techniques and ideas on psi phenomena as an extension of normal intimacy.

My continued dialogue with Ernest Lawrence Rossi has provided much material over the years, both for thought and, occasionally, for publication. This is the second book in which I've discussed his model of a self-reflectiveness scale for dreams. This is a significant contribution to dream research that I hope becomes widely accepted.

William Sulis has been generous in allowing me to share his cutting-edge thought on the concept of "saliency," before he has published a major work on the subject. I believe that this work on the mathematics of an archetypal universe will have far-reaching consequences for science.

FROM THE INSIDE OUT

The Creator gathered all of creation and said, "I want to hide
something from the humans until they are ready for it. It is
the realization that they create their own reality." The eagle
said, "Give it to me, I will take it to the moon." The Creator
said, "No, one day they will go there and find it." The salmon
said, "I will hide it on the bottom of the ocean." "No. They
will go there, too." The buffalo said, "I will bury it on the
great plains." The Creator said, "They will cut into the skin
of the earth and find it even there." Then Grandmother Mole,
who lives in the breast of Mother Earth, and who has no
physical eyes, but sees with spiritual eyes, said, "Put it inside
them."
  And the Creator said, "It is done."
                    —Gary Zukav quoting a Native American[1]

We've grown used to thinking that things happen to us
from the outside-in. We are small and the world is
large. At birth we are assumed to be simple creatures
who gradually look and hear, and smell and touch, thus slowly
accumulating all that which we come to know. We supposedly
learn behavior by rote, simply repeating the actions of others until they are also stored away, available for future use. At some
point, we have stored away enough memories and behaviors that
we can begin to rationally process them. From that point on, we
use our elegant minds—which supposedly separate us from the
rest of the animal kingdom—to think things over and make logical decisions. We like that image of ourselves—as rational beings
in control of our own destinies. The world is outside us and we

---

[1] Gary Zukav, in "What is the Soul?" in *Life Magazine,* December 1997.

are limited by that world, but as rational beings we are able to deal with the challenges it presents us.

In this view, everything happens from the outside-in. This book is going to express a heresy: everything actually happens from the inside-out! At birth, we are not simple creatures; we are complex repositories of memories and behaviors. When we look and hear, and smell and touch, we are not simply pulling in from the outside, we are reaching out from the inside. While we may have to learn some behavior by rote, others are already stored away, awaiting "triggers" that release them.

When it comes to making decisions, we don't think things over and make logical decisions. Instead, there seems to be something inside that already knows who we are and who we will become. In order to get to that person we are intended to become, inside things are churning away, playing with possibilities. We get a peek into the process when we remember a dream. In fact, dreams are the main way that the inner makes its way into the outer.

Dreams are not the only way, however. Sometimes, something going on inside us coincides with something going on outside in a dramatic way. We think about someone we love and, at just that moment, the phone rings and the person we love is on the line. We usually dismiss this as coincidence, yet more often it is something inside wanting to come out. Only, in such cases, the inside has to be much bigger than our personal inside; it has to be big enough to include the whole world and all who are in it.

Sometimes we need tools to help the inside come out. Our ancestors, foolish, superstitious beings that they were (in the *traditional* modern view, I stress), developed divinatory tools to help the inside reveal itself to the outside, tools like the I Ching or the Tarot deck or rune stones or astrology, or a vast number of other divinatory devices that capture patterns existing both inside and outside at the same time.

When something wants to come out from within, it's going to find a way, and sometimes that way may not fit our preconceptions. So, first of all, we have to be open enough and flexible enough to accept what comes and not dismiss it just because it doesn't fit, or just because it makes us feel uncomfortable. Second, we have to be willing to simply accept the experience and whatever it does for and to us without rushing into putting it into a "box" that explains it all away. Finally, we have to slowly digest the experience, integrating it into who we are and what we believe. We need to take time with this process as the experience is more important than the understanding.

From the inside out—that sounds strange to us, but the world is often stranger than we could ever imagine. This book looks at that inside-out world. Hopefully, by the end of the book, you will recognize it as the world in which we all live.

FINDING OUR MYTH AND FULFILLING OUR DESTINY

> It is only our conscious mind that does not know; the unconscious seems already informed, and to have submitted the case to a careful prognostic examination, more or less in the way consciousness would have done if it had known the relevant facts. But, precisely because they were subliminal, they could be perceived by the unconscious and submitted to a sort of examination that anticipates their ultimate result.[2]

Psychologist C. G. Jung insisted that we each need to discover our particular myth. If that sounds like a strange way to express the need to discover our destiny, it is because we have lost our connection with myth. Myths are not simply made-up stories about gods and goddesses, monsters and treasures, adventures and quests. Those gods and goddesses represent eternal human qualities that still live in each of us. Those monsters represent the all-too-human monsters we struggle with in our own lives; the treasures are those things we prize above all else. Each of our lives is filled with adventure if we see it through the right lens. Each of us is engaged in a quest that determines not only the course of our own individual lives, but the course of all lives. The world is filled with meaning and we need to find ways to connect with that meaning, in order to discover our personal myth; i.e., why we are here on this earth.

We have deep roots that intertwine with the roots of all creatures in all times. We are each manifestations of a single guiding principle, a single meaning that struggles to make itself known. When we look closely enough at the world around us,

---

[2] C. G. Jung, *The Structure and Dynamics of the Psyche*, Collected Works, vol. 8. Bollingen Series XX, 2nd. ed. (Princeton: Princeton University Press, 1969), ¶545.

we see ourselves looking back. When we dig deep enough into our own identity, we see the whole world spread before us.

What I'm saying is truth, esoteric truth, hidden truth, taught by all spiritual and occult traditions. All too often, even those in the traditions might not recognize them. It is far too easy to get lost in the details of a given tradition and lose sight of the few essential truths that lie hidden within the myriads of details specific to a given tradition. But all traditions know that we are one. All know that it is possible to experience that oneness. All know that life itself has a purpose and that we each have a purpose within the greater purpose.

Though there are many ways to say this, throughout this book I will most often emphasize just two. First, I will talk about the ways these strange events are experienced in each of our lives, because at some level, the only things we really accept are those which we have experienced ourselves. Second, I will bring in scientific descriptions of unusual phenomena, simply because we are all so inculcated with the view that science knows everything (or so we think), that it's hard for us to take anything truly unusual seriously unless it has scientific support.

Beyond that, I will give everyone free rein to include a wide variety of both fact and fiction in support of these claims. Though I'll try to be careful to indicate which is which, I can't guarantee which we will find to be more true. Personally I have found as much truth in fiction as in fact.

THE PSYCHOID NATURE OF REALITY

> Perhaps through our cells, or through the general cohesiveness of sentience and matter, we have access to *any* information in the universe.[3]

Jung's self-exploration, work with patients, and study of mythology all combined to make him realize that there were two progressively larger strata beneath consciousness: 1) the personal unconscious (where personal memories that we have either repressed or simply never brought into consciousness are

---

[3] Richard Grossinger, "The Dream Work," in Richard A. Russo, *Dreams are Wiser than Men* (Berkeley: North Atlantic Books, 1987), p. 212.

stored); and 2) the collective unconscious (where the entire history of the evolution of consciousness appears to be stored). The collective unconscious is nothing mystical. Our bodies themselves are a virtual storehouse of the entire history of life leading up to present day humanity. All living creatures at birth already have a wealth of behavioral possibilities stored in the brain and body. If not, they would never survive. As the level of complexity of animals rises, the complexity and subtlety of the inherited behaviors (or possibilities of behaviors) grows. Undoubtedly at the same point in time when dreams came into existence (as we will find later, this was a minimum of 65 million years ago!), the ability to access information symbolically also was stored, so we now have access to not only inherited behaviors, but to inherited symbolic behaviors!

But even that isn't the whole story. Strange as it sounds, it appears that the world itself is made up neither of matter, nor of mind, but of something that either partakes of both, or is more primary than either. Jung, who was ahead of his time in this area, as in so many others, called this underlying reality the *Unus Mundus*, the unitary reality. But he also came up with another coinage late in his life which is even more useful. Since this unus mundus partakes both of matter and of psyche, yet transcends both, Jung termed it *psychoid*.

Jung was a *depth psychologist*; quite literally, one who explores the depths of the psyche. He found that at its depths, the psyche had no limits in time or space. He was very interested in the fact that when physicists went deeply enough into matter, what they found no longer had any characteristics we associate with matter. In fact, they often were forced to bring in consciousness as a major constituent of reality. Because of this confluence of interests, Jung and physicist Wolfgang Pauli[4] together looked for a neutral language that could be used for this psychoid reality. Though, like most pioneers, they weren't

---

[4] Wolfgang Pauli won the Nobel Prize in 1945 for his discovery of the exclusion principle in physics, in which no two electrons in an atom can have the same quantum state. Pauli went through a Jungian analysis with a colleague of Jung's. Jung wrote about Pauli's dreams, without mentioning Pauli by name, in "Individual Dream Symbolism in Relation to Alchemy," included in C. G. Jung, Collected Works, vol. 12: 2nd ed.: *Psychology and Alchemy*, Bollingen Series XX (Princeton: Princeton University Press, 1968), pp. 39–224.

wholly successful, they laid some tracks in the wilderness which all of us can follow.

One discovery was that this psychoid reality had structure. It was composed of nearly timeless elements Jung termed *archetypes*. These were structures that underlie everything we experience either inside or outside ourselves. The archetypes are the gods and goddesses, monsters and treasures, adventures and quests that I said earlier still live inside us. But archetypes are also the mundane structures through which we see all the people and things and actions of the world around us. Because they are the constituents of the psychoid world, they are not limited by the constraints of time or place. Whenever we experience something that doesn't seem to conform to the normal "laws of science," we can usually assume that there are archetypal roots to our experience. This book will argue that whenever we encounter the anomalous, we should look for the archetypal meaning that is attempting to be expressed. We will see this most clearly in our later discussion of *synchronicity*, dreams, and other less obvious places.

THE INFINITE SPHERE

It [i.e., Nature, or the Universe, or perhaps even God] is an infinite sphere, the center of which is everywhere, the circumference nowhere.[5]

The archetype of the individual is the Self. The Self is all embracing. God is a circle whose center is everywhere and whose circumference is nowhere."[6]

Most of us still believe in a Newtonian world made up of separate material "things." Imagine the things of the world as a set of children's blocks. In this Newtonian view, everything can be made by piling our blocks together in different arrangements.

---

[5] Jorge Luis Borges, "Pascal's Sphere," in *Other Inquisitions: 1937–1952* (New York: Washington Square Press, 1966), p. 8.

[6] C. G. Jung, comments on Ira Progoff's doctoral dissertation, in William McGuire, ed., *C. G. Jung Speaking: Interviews and Encounters*, Bollingen Series XCVII (Princeton: Princeton University Press, 1977), p. 216.

Every event in this world is supposedly caused by an action of some material "thing." In such a world, it becomes increasingly natural to also think of ourselves as "things." But the world is actually not much like this now-outmoded scientific picture.

The years 1900–1930 brought about a nearly total overturn of this Newtonian worldview. First came a series of discoveries that showed that the supposed smallest "things" of the world — atoms — were not the smallest things at all. Instead they contained still smaller particles, separated by enormous relative distances. Then came Einstein with the special Theory of Relativity, which revealed that the only absolute in our universe was the speed of light, hardly a thing. Then his general Theory of Relativity, which showed that all motion is relative to the observer; we are ineluctably intertwined with the world around us. Further, that space and time were not separate entities; rather, that reality is a giant space-time continuum.

Then came quantum mechanics, which further tore away any "thinginess" which was left for reality. At present, most physicists presume that the basic building blocks of reality are neither atoms, nor subatomic particles, but *quarks*, which have qualities that can only be described mathematically. In this quantum world, cause-and-effect no longer have meaning; rather things come into, or pass out of, existence based on probabilities, not certainties. Like the local weatherman, who never says it's going to rain, just that there is a 60 percent chance of rain, quantum mechanics doesn't tell us that a certain particle will come into existence in a certain reaction; just that there is a 20 percent chance it will. In the most commonly accepted model of reality, based on quantum mechanics,[7] there is no reality as we know it until the act of observation takes place, which actualizes the probability and creates the seemingly solid world around us.

In the 1940s, this revolution in worldview moved from physics to biology and neurophysiology. Famed neurophysiologist Karl Lashley tried to discover the "atoms" of memory — *engrams*, as he termed them — the sites where specific memories are stored in the brain. Instead he found that he could cut out

---

[7] The Copenhagen Interpretation was originally developed by Niels Bohr as a philosophical description of quantum mechanics.

half a rat's brain, any half, and the rat could still perform relatively normally. His assistant at the time, now equally famed — Karl Pribram — realized that this could only mean that memories are not stored in specific locations, like books in a library. Instead they have to be stored within the total pattern of the brain. And that pattern has to be *holographic*; any part of the brain must contain the whole pattern, though perhaps an increasingly fuzzy pattern as more and more of the brain is destroyed. It wasn't until much later that Pribram had the realization that all reality must be holographic! Instead of "things," reality must be made up of waves forming patterns, and every piece of that reality must contain, at least potentially, all patterns in much the same way that a visual hologram does.

THE ROLE OF THE INDIVIDUAL

To describe reality we must describe the things that exist, and a description of conscious entities includes a description of their inner worlds. And the interior decorating of a human being, even when it includes a consciousness of world out there, will be lush with particulars not to be found out there.[8]

But let's return to the role of the individual in this strange unitary world. If the inner and outer worlds are inextricably intertwined, if, in fact, they are a single world, then the role of the individual becomes critical in understanding and advancing that world. It is possible to come to an understanding of this ultimate reality either by looking outward at the physical world and describing carefully what we see, or equally by looking inward at the world of the psyche and describing carefully what we experience. That latter has the advantage that, at least in part, our entry into that world is unique to each of us. We each have a window into eternity. We are each the center of "an infinite sphere, the center of which is everywhere, the circumference nowhere."

---

[8] Rebecca Goldstein, *The Mind-Body Problem* (New York: Random House, 1983), p. 153.

The great Greek thinkers approached truth through *a priori* premises, dialectical argument, and logical extrapolation. It never occurred to them that they needed to check their conclusions against reality. For example, Aristotle concluded from logical reasoning that a heavy object fell faster than a light object. But neither he nor any of those who followed and repeated his conclusion ever tried to see if, in fact, this was true. It wasn't until the Renaissance that we began to look around us, describe carefully what we saw, and test our conclusions in reality. Just as Aristotle was representative of the earlier approach, Leonardo da Vinci can be seen as representative of the Renaissance ideal, making statements such as, "Experience never errs; it is only your judgements that err by promising themselves such as are not caused by your experiments."[9]

By turning our gaze outward on physical reality, inevitably we came to see ourselves in the privileged position of observer. Just as it never occurred to the Greeks to doubt the limits of pure reason, it never occurred to Renaissance thinkers that it might be impossible to separate the act of observation from the object under observation. But just as relativity and quantum mechanics showed the limits of Newtonian mechanics, they also revealed that observation is relative, and that it is ultimately impossible to isolate ourselves from our observations. Physicist John Wheeler summarized this succinctly by saying that "man as observer changed into man as participator."[10]

Similarly the discoveries of the mind, ranging from those of neurophysiology to clinical psychology, brought about the further recognition that each of us constructs our own version of reality within ourselves. Jung added a further twist with his discovery of archetypes that structure both physical and psychic reality. Since we are all born with access to archetypes that underlie total reality, we each possess a series of common windows out onto reality. Jung also pointed out that archetypes are content-free; that is, they are like naked dressing-room dummies awaiting experience to clothe them. Through the lens of

---

[9] Jean Paul Richter, *The Notebooks of Leonardo da Vinci*, 2 vols. (New York: Dover Publications, 1970), p. 288.

[10] John A. Wheeler, K. S. Thorne, and C. Misner, *Gravitation* (San Francisco: W. H. Freeman & Co., 1973), p. 1273. Add to bibliography.

archetypes, we can all experience the same abstract reality, yet our individual experience of that reality is unique to each of us, defined by our particular strengths and weaknesses, colored by our individual experiences. We each serve as a unique filter for reality.

But perhaps our role is more significant still. Jung thought so. As we descend ever deeper into the psyche, we eventually arrive at a place that can only be described in mystical terms. Since a sufficient number of people, in a sufficient number of disparate spiritual traditions, have reached is depth, we can even chart its stages. First, there is a state of total bliss, which is experienced as a union with all reality, yet in which somehow, paradoxically, we still retain our individual sense of identity. This stage is regarded as sort of a kindergarten of transcendence, a starting place from which we can proceed toward deeper understanding. We might call that the world of the archetypes.

The next great state is much harder to describe, and fewer have reached it. Western mystic Franklin Merrell-Wolff has termed it aptly "The Place of High Indifference." At this stage, there is no longer any sense of bliss, or in fact any emotion as such. Though we still have a sense of identity, identity no longer has any particular meaning. Things are simply complete in and of themselves, and we, as both part of, and all of, those things, are ourselves complete.

But there are still deeper layers. Chinese Buddhists have captured the process of enlightenment in a series of ten drawings showing the stages a young ox-herder goes through in search of his lost ox. There are several versions of this series, which are best known in the Western world through D. T. Suzuki's *Manual of Zen Buddhism*.[11] In one version the last stage is represented by a simple circle that fills the page, with the caption "Both vanished"; this might be regarded as "The Place of High Indifference." But other versions of the ox-herder pictures go two stages further. After "Both vanished" (called "The ox and the man both gone out of sight" in one version), there is a stage called "Returning to the origin, back to the source," which

---

[11] D. T. Suzuki, *Manual of Zen Buddhism* (London: Rider, 1950).

shows the natural world, symbolized by a stark tree above rocks. Then finally a stage called "Entering the city with bliss-bestowing hands," where the young ox-herder meets an old, fat, jovial master. Both are clearly wanderers with no fixed abode, but there is a lovely, leafy tree over their heads. In other words, after all the stages of enlightenment, finally one comes back to the world to help others. And, in the process, we meet ourselves, both as young and naive and as old and wise.

Jung called the wise old man or woman within each of us the *Self*, capitalizing the word to separate it from our normal sense of "self." Since we encounter the entire world through the lens of the archetypes, even divinity must be met through an archetype. We can trace the evolution of the Self by looking at humanity's image of the godhead at key stages in history. The gods don't change over time; our archetype of divinity changes. (It is important to remember that this is a psychological issue, not a metaphysical issue; i.e., it has nothing to do with the actual existence or non-existence of divinity; our views are necessarily limited by the archetypal structures within us, which change very slowly, as with any other evolutionary change.)

For the ancient Greeks, divinity had a very human character because they were not yet able to imagine divinity wholly separate and distinct from human characteristics. The gods were personifications of representative human types—father/Zeus, mother/Hera, warrior/Ares, beauty/Aphrodite, trickery/Hermes, etc. Though the gods lived in their own realm on Olympus, they frequently came down to Earth and interacted with men and women: drinking, mating, interfering in our affairs as they chose. Men and women were powerless against these all-too-human, yet infinitely powerful gods.

The Jews were the first culture to believe in a single all-powerful god—Jehovah—who transcended human characteristics. He (for the godhead was, at this stage viewed as masculine) created the world and all in it, and then largely left humanity to its own devices. There were, however, still traces of the more primitive view of divinity. For example, Jehovah still occasionally interceded in human affairs: turning Lot's wife into a pillar of salt; causing the great flood, leaving only Noah's ark to survive; or parting the Red Sea for the Jews to escape their Egyptian masters. Largely though, Jehovah only communicated with a few chosen humans—such as Moses or Jacob—and then only through intermediate symbols such as a burning bush or an angel.

With Christianity, a further step was taken in the evolution of divinity. For the first time, a divinity could be contained within a human being (as opposed to divinity having human characteristics, as with the Greeks, or divinity being wholly separate from humanity, as with the Jews). Christ was something new: both human and divine. He provided an example of how the human and the divine can live together within a single being. (As did Buddha when he appeared in the East five hundred years earlier.)

Only now are ordinary men and women awakening to that same realization: that each of us possesses divinity, if we are willing to look within and find it. If we do that, however, we find ourselves torn—like Christ and Buddha—between our human nature and our divine nature. By living with that tension, we not only advance ourselves spiritually, but we also help advance the archetype of divinity—the Self.

An important role indeed! In this book, we will examine at length the ways in which we experience that inner world: through dreams, through synchronistic events through meditation and active imagination, and through the use of divinatory tools, such as the I Ching. On the way, we will move back-and-forth between those personal experiences and what they tell us about the unitary world within which they occur. Let us begin with part of the inner world that we all have experienced, but all too often ignore—our dreams.

DREAMS

*Among the many puzzles of medical psychology there is one
problem child, the dream.*

—C. G. Jung.[1]

*In a certain sense, dreams are realer than life. That is, they
are closer to the roots of our being than daily waking events.
If we exist in some ultimate terms, it is beyond the senses and
beyond consciousness.*

—Richard Grossinger.[2]

Dreams are a gateway to a source of information and
support deeper than consciousness. Especially significant are those dreams where oracular voices come out
of nowhere giving advice or instruction. Anyone who has ever
had such a dream can sympathize with our ancestors who felt
that they were hearing a message from the gods. If, in our time,
the gods now live inside our psyches, their messages are no less
important to heed. In my own experience, these dreams are very
rare. In one such dream, a voice that had to be honored told me
that there are two great things to obtain. First are *gateways*. Second are *rituals*.

[1] C. G. Jung, "On the Nature of Dreams," in *The Structure and Dynamics of the
Psyche,* Collected Works, vol. 8: Bollingen Series XX, 2nd ed. (Princeton:
Princeton University Press, 1969), ¶ 531.
[2] Richard Grossinger, "The Dream Work," in Richard A. Russo, *Dreams are
Wiser than Men* (Berkeley: North Atlantic Books, 1987), p. 204.

The *American Heritage Dictionary* defines a gateway as "an opening or a structure framing an opening that may be closed by a gate," and also as "something that serves as an entrance or means of access." And the example provided is, tellingly, metaphorical: "a gateway to success."

A wall divides the world into two parts. As long as we are on one side of the wall, there is no way of discovering what is on the other side unless we find a gateway through which we can pass. A gateway provides an entrance, an access to something new. And also note that the gateway may be regarded as simply the "structure framing an opening"; that is, we see a structure and then look within it for the opening to something new. So my dream says that the first thing we all need are openings, entrances, methods of access that allow us to either pass beyond the world as we know it, or at least to see beyond that world into different worlds. Dreams are one gateway, but we will find other gateways along the way.

The same dictionary defines ritual as "the prescribed form or order of conducting a religious or solemn ceremony," and also as "a detailed method of procedure faithfully or regularly followed." So once we find a gateway, we need to adopt a "detailed method of procedure" that we must follow "regularly" and "faithfully." And we must approach this procedure with a "solemn," even "religious" attitude!

Figure 1. A gateway provides an entrance, an access to something new. (Reprinted from *Grafton's Naughty French Spot Illustrations*.)

At their most elemental, rituals are merely repeated actions. If we ignore the need for solemnity, a ritual can be simply a robot-like repetition of something that we have done so many times before that we no longer need to think about it. For example, the nighttime ritual we go through each day in preparation for bed, in which we automatically brush our teeth, wash our face, put on our pajamas, all in a known order and manner. At this level, rituals are functional. At its highest level, a ritual might be the body of rites used in a religious ceremony. Here rituals pass beyond function to spirituality. By going through the steps of spiritual rituals in the prescribed order, we hope to experience a reality that transcends normal experience.

Most importantly, we *construct* rituals. We try out possibilities until we discover a set that works, then it becomes a ritual. We might not be aware that we are ritualizing a process, but it is still our actions that create the ritual. While gateways come from a deeper source inside us, it is up to us to construct the rituals necessary to make proper use of those gateways. The process of dreaming is, itself, a magnificent gateway to the inner world. In fact, each dream can be a unique gateway into some aspect of both our life and the larger impersonal world that lies both inside and outside. But first we need to create general rituals for dealing with dreams, then we can use those rituals to explore the many and varied vistas revealed by individual dreams. And some of these dreams may be important enough to force us to construct new rituals for our lives.

Let's begin with the larger ritual of how to deal with our dreams. There are three main stages to this ritual: first we learn to remember our dreams, next we learn how to honor them, and finally, we learn how to interpret them (where necessary). This chapter will present powerful dreams (gateways), and help provide readers with techniques that have been of use to others when dealing with dreams (rituals). Readers should feel free to personalize these rituals until they fit comfortably.

REMEMBERING OUR DREAMS

To describe the remembering of dreams as an art is partially a confession of the mystery of the process. Yet, in many respects, learning to recall dreams is

similar to learning any other skill: it requires motiva-
tion, an especially adapted vigilant strategy, an over-
coming of possible resistance, and, above all, an
attitude of confident patience.[3]

Let me tell you a story from the life of psychologist and dream
pioneer Dr. Henry Reed where he made use of all the traits he
mentions above—especially "confident patience." Thirty years
ago, before he was Dr. Reed, while Henry was studying psychology in graduate school, he made a decision to try and remember his dreams. He had reached an impasse in his life and
had become an alcoholic, though he couldn't yet admit this to
himself. Somehow he knew that dreams could help him.

Often, in times of crisis, we know from some deeper source
within us that we need to do something. But far too often we
don't heed the quiet inner voice. Henry did. He went to the
trouble of constructing a handmade journal to hold his dreams.
He wrote a prayer in the journal asking for a dream to help him
in his time of need, then laid it beside his bed. Despite this conscious effort to produce dreams, they didn't come. Not that
night, nor the next, nor the one after that. In fact it was over
three months before a dream came to him, a dream that would
change his life.

In a dream, Henry was camping in a tent in a sacred
sanctuary belonging to a Wise Old Man.[4] He looked
around his beautiful rural surroundings and was dis-
gusted to see an empty bottle of wine lying by a hay-
stack. He indignantly told the Wise Old Man that there
must be a drunk squatting on the land. He suggested
strongly that they should kick him out immediately.
The Wise Old Man looked kindly at Henry, but told him
that he regarded the drunk as his friend, and that he
had used the wine to tempt him to come there so that he
could be fed.

---

[3] Henry Reed, "The Art of Remembering Dreams," *Quadrant* (Summer, 1996), p. 48.
[4] In the introduction, I mentioned that there is a source of deep wisdom inside
us that Jung found was often personified by a Wise Old Man (or a Wise Old
Woman, depending on our gender).

When Henry looked around to see what kind of food the Wise Old Man had left for the drunk—health food, he wondered?—all he saw was an empty jar of mayonnaise and an empty bag of potato chips. Confused by this strange food and shamed by the contrast between his sanctimonious self-righteousness and the Wise Old Man's compassion, Henry left the Wise Old Man and went back to his own tent.

It was several years before Dr. Reed (as he was now known) was to finally understand that seminal dream. At the time of the dream, all he had understood about it was that he was probably the drunk and that perhaps he needed to be less harsh with himself in dealing with his drinking problem. That was quite a lot to learn; before the dream he hadn't been willing to admit that he was an alcoholic, and yet he despised himself for being one. We are often in such paradoxical situations in our lives.

Figure 2. We have to listen closely if we're going to hear the quiet voice from within (reprinted from *Grafton's Humorous Victorian Spot Illustrations*).

He also knew that he needed to learn all that he could about dreams. So while he finished his doctorate and began teaching, he read all that he could about dreams and kept his dream journal by his bed. Though at first progress continued to be slow, very gradually his ability to remember dreams improved. Unfortunately his drinking problem got worse. Another dream, which we won't discuss here, helped him decide to go into psychotherapy with a Jungian analyst. While he waited for a first session, he began attending Alcoholics Anonymous meetings. Then one night, when he stopped at a liquor store for a bottle of liquor, he found that he just couldn't pick it up. Something deep inside wouldn't let him. He went home sad and empty of spirit, but sober.

His dream research continued. He was fascinated by the healing dreams incubated by the ancient Greeks at the temple of Asclepius, the legendary Greek physician and, later, god of healing. People would come to the temple, much as someone today would make a pilgrimage to Mecca or to Lourdes. There they would perform spiritual rituals to honor Asclepius, and sleep in the temple, hoping for a healing dream from the god. Not only did many receive dreams diagnosing their problems and suggesting cures, many were actually healed during the night, seemingly by the dreams. The first such temple originated in Epidaurus in about 380 B.C. and was so popular that similar temples appeared all over Greece, reaching their peak in numbers at somewhere between 200 and 400 temples in the second century. So people came to the temples of Asclepius for five hundred years!

In modern times it is always fashionable to assume that our ancestors were simply credulous fools duped by the trickery of the temple priests. This is the view, for example, of Professor Charles Singer in his *Short History of Medicine*. In contrast, a mammoth scholarly study by Emma J. and Ludwig Edelstein concluded that "the ancients were hardly so easy to fool that a mummery performed daily in hundreds of places throughout the centuries would never have been detected or suspected or at least hinted at."[5] Perhaps we would be better to defer our judgment of ancient rituals until we have been more successful in constructing modern rituals of healing and spiritual transformation.

---

[5] See Edwin Diamond, *The Science of Dreams* (London: Eyre & Spottiswoode, 1962), pp. 211–213.

Dr. Reed decided that he would attempt to recreate a similar situation, where people could come to a sacred site hoping to incubate healing dreams. We can see that in selecting such a project, he was taking the first steps toward himself becoming a Wise Old Man who could help heal others. He obtained funding, then located people interested in participating in this project. He selected an outdoor setting—like his dream, though that wasn't in his mind at the time. There would be a dome-shaped "dream tent," which would serve as a sanctuary, where someone could seek a healing dream. Again, in selecting a tent, he was recreating part of his dream without realizing it.

After he arrived at the camp and set up the dream tent, however, he started to feel insecure, even ridiculous. What a stupid idea this was! How could he possibly ask people to go along with it? He decided not to say this was a sacred place to incubate healing dreams and instead to merely refer to the tent as "a fun place to sleep if you wanted to get away from the crowd and focus on your dreams." Just then, when he was ready to retreat from his vision, just as he had retreated in his dream years before, he remembered a joke from childhood. Maybe you heard it once yourself and went "yuck." Here's the way it goes:

> There was a man with a loathsome skin disease. His body was covered with pus-filled scabs which he would pick off and put into a bag. The pus was drained and stored in a jar. Both bag and jar were stored in a closet in his house. One day, when he was away on vacation, a friend wandered into his house and somehow locked himself in the closet. When the man returned from vacation a week later, the man inside the closet heard him and began calling out for help. The man let his friend out of the closet and told him that he had been lucky to survive. His friend agreed, saying that, "I would have starved if it hadn't been for the potato chips and mayonnaise."

Now that's a pretty disgusting joke, but it opened Dr. Reed's eyes. Suddenly he knew the meaning of his dream. Beneath the disgusting image of the joke is a picture of a man feeding on the products of illness. In Dr. Reed's dream, the Wise Old Man had tempted the drunk with wine, then fed him "potato chips and mayonnaise," i.e., he had fed him his own illness as its own cure. In Henry's life, after he had the dream, he accepted his alcoholism and lived with it for several years. The Wise Old Man inside him had known that it was important for Henry to accept his alcoholism as part of who he was, to feed it to himself, so to speak. That was all that was necessary in order for him to survive. During the several years since he originally had the dream, in the dark of the closet, deep inside, a "friend" was feeding on his disease. Without Henry ever being aware of it, he was being healed *from the inside out.* Now that he was healed, it was time for him to help heal others. But first he had to know that he was healed. He had to "come out of the closet," as the gay community has so vividly pictured their own admission of gay identity. So he unconsciously re-created the dream setting and allowed the dream's meaning to emerge into consciousness.

Oh yes, and Dr. Reed did go ahead with using the dream tent to incubate dreams—with great success! It led to a whole series of rich encounters with dreams that were recorded in *The Sundance Journal.* The dream incubation work was just the beginning of this process.

This need to honor our illness, our wound, is one of the most important ways we can begin to heal ourselves. Those who are willing to go through this process often become healers themselves. They are known as "wounded healers," since it is by healing their own wound that they develop the ability to help others heal themselves.

Another dreamer who was in the process of divorcing her husband had the following dream that has a similar message.

She lived in the upstairs portion of a house with her husband. A man, who in real life had worked for her, in the dream lived and worked downstairs. As the dream began, she told her husband that all he had to do was to go downstairs.

Now the worker had somehow originally burned a hole in his finger. The wound became his primary business. Every day he applied glue to the hole; somehow, as long as he did this, he could make the business run. But now, the dream said, it was time to take off the scab that had formed.

When the scab was removed, the impurity that was still underneath the skin came out of the finger as well. The dreamer knew it was time to stop applying the glue every day and let the wound heal for good.

Now this dream might not be quite as easy to follow as Dr. Reed's, but the worker is the key. While the woman and her husband have lived upstairs—that is, she's been consciously dealing with her husband—down below, in the unconscious part of her mind, work has been going on—healing work. The worker there has a hole burned in his finger, just as she had a wound burnt inside her by the difficulties caused by her marriage. Every day, in the unconscious, this worker is gluing the hole closed, keeping it from overflowing into her life. That is his work—his "business."

But the dream tells her that now it's time to take off the scab. When it is removed, the "impurity," the burning wound she felt inside her, comes out as well. So now there is no further need to glue up the hole each day. It's time for the husband to come downstairs and see that the healing is complete.

Let's return to the general question of remembering our dreams. Jung discovered that our unconscious mind is independent of our conscious control. Yet it is aware of our conscious attitude and, in fact, it treats us as we treat it. If we are indifferent to our dreams, we aren't likely to remember them. If we honor them, they become easier to remember. When I first started in therapy, the Jungian-oriented therapist told me that we would be working a great deal with dreams. When I explained that I never dreamed, he suggested that, nevertheless, it would be wise to keep a notebook and pencil by my bed in case I did remember a dream. So that night, I laid a pencil and stenographer's pad by my bed, then went to sleep. I had five dreams! From that day until now, twenty years later, I have remembered and recorded an average of three dreams a night, over 20,000 dreams to date.

In contrast, look at Dr. Reed's experience. He didn't just buy a notebook from the store, as I did. He went to the trouble of making a personal dream journal, then composing a special prayer asking for healing dreams. Yet it was still three months before he dreamed. Imagine the perseverance it took to hold to his resolve over those three months. The same sort of perseverance of spirit would eventually enable him to become sober again.

Most people's experience lies somewhere between Dr. Reed's and my own. Even if they, like the two of us, don't normally remember dreams, the mere intention of remembering them is enough to remember a dream. It is important, however, to make it as easy as possible to record the dream because dreams fade from consciousness very quickly.

Dreaming has traditionally been thought to be characterized by rapid eye movement (REM), though it is known that "some dreaming does occur in [non-REM] sleep as well."[6] More recently, research by Dr. Alan Moffitt, in his dream laboratory in Ottawa, Canada, has demonstrated conclusively that dreaming is not limited to the REM stage of sleep.[7] Dream recall is, however, better during REM sleep, which may have misled earlier researchers. Dr. Moffitt remarks that:

> The reason that we and other researchers have not found clear and distinct correlates of the states of the brain associated with dreaming and not dreaming may be because *there are none*. In my opinion, our data indicate that dreaming is continuous throughout sleep.[8]

Since we seem to be dreaming continuously during the night, we are likely to be dreaming at the moment we wake. At that moment, we are in the twilight phase of consciousness that lies between sleep and waking. If we move too quickly into the routine of the day, the dreams vanish. Even body movement is enough to shift from that twilight phase, so stay in the reverie for a moment and see if there is a dream floating at the edge of consciousness. If so, try and let it remember itself (that's closer to the actuality than our consciously trying to remember it, which doesn't tend to be very effective), record it immediately; though we may feel confident at the time that we will later re-

---

[6] Steven Rose, *The Conscious Brain* (New York: Vintage Books, 1976), p. 303.

[7] See Alan Moffitt, "The Creation of Self in Dreaming and Waking," *Psychological Perspectives*, Issue 30 (Los Angeles: C. G. Jung Institute, 1994), pp. 42–69. For more details of the research, see Sheila Purcell, Alan Moffitt, and Robert Hoffman, "Waking, Dreaming, and Self-Regulation," in Alan Moffitt, Milton Kramer, and Robert Hoffman (editors), *The Functions of Dreaming* (Albany: State University of New York Press, 1993), pp. 197–260.

[8] Alan Moffitt, "The Creation of Self in Dreaming and Waking," p. 47.

member it, it is still only stored in short-term memory and will often vanish entirely as the day goes on.

I myself soon shifted from a pad and a pencil to a micro-cassette recorder. That way, I didn't have to turn on the light in order to record the dream; I just had to mumble into the recorder (and it often is just a mumble, sometimes unfortunately an unintelligible mumble). In the morning, I type the dreams into a word-processor. I've long ago set-up a special word-processing format for dreams, with a small typeface such that when I print it, I can cut out the printed portion and scotch-tape it into a stenographer's pad for permanent printed storage. (I've recently filled my 81st such notebook.) By typing my dreams into the word-processor, they are also stored in the computer. I can then use the computer's ability to index all the words in the dreams, so that later I can look up any dreams in which a particular image occurs. This is especially useful since the elements of dreams are often best understood by following them through a sequence of dreams over an extended period of time.

In no way, however, should you judge the efficacy of your dream-work by the sheer number of dreams you remember and record. For some people like me, it's important to remember a great number of dreams. Others, equally convinced of the value of dreams, seem to have an inner filtering process that allows only the most memorable dreams to emerge into consciousness. For them, remembering too many dreams can get in the way of reflecting properly on a few key ones. At one point in my own life, a voice in a dream told me that I should stop recording my dreams. And, as we have already seen, when that voice speaks, you listen. So I totally stopped recording dreams. During this period of time, though I would still sometimes remember dreams in the morning, the number I remembered dropped dramatically. When I did remember a dream, I would simply go over it in my mind, then I'd just let it go. After about ten months, I suddenly became aware that it was time to once more record my dreams. I can't say just how I knew that, I just did. Again this is an example of listening to the quiet voice from within.

My dream life immediately returned to its normal frequency of about three dreams remembered per night. That went on for several years, then one year the frequency went down drastically. In the first three months, I only remembered three dreams. During the rest of the year, I remembered less than three per month! Rather than worrying, I assumed that there was a purpose, and simply accepted the new state of things. As a new year began, my dreams once more returned to their normal frequency. The whole process is a mystery that we should honor.

To summarize this section, the important elements in remembering your dreams are: 1) the desire to remember them; 2) actually recording them. Before I describe how to honor dreams, let us look at the relationship between the dream state and the waking state.

TIBETAN BARDOS AND LEVELS OF SELF-REFLECTION IN THE DREAM STATE

For years, ever since it was first published [in 1927], the *Bardo Thödol* [an alternative title for *The Tibetan Book of the Dead*] has been my constant companion, and to it I owe not only many stimulating ideas and discoveries but also many fundamental insights.[9]

The *Tibetan Book of the Dead*[10] is a Tibetan Buddhist guide about death and dying; it records the three successive states — *bardos* — that the soul passes through between dying and being reborn. Jung thought highly of it as a document describing the progressive depths of the collective unconscious. Of particular interest to us, the bardos can also be seen as describing the phases of sleep and dreaming. In his *Tibetan Book of Living and Dying*, Sogyal Rinpoche compares the three bardos to the three stages of sleep: 1) falling asleep; 2) dreaming; and 3) the twilight stage between waking and dreaming.

---

[9] C. G. Jung, "Psychological Commentary on *The Tibetan Book of the Dead*," in *Psychology and Religion: West and East*, Collected Works, vol. 11: Bollingen Series XX, 2nd ed. (Princeton: Princeton University Press, 1969), ¶ 833.
[10] W. Y. Evans-Wentz, ed., *The Tibetan Book of the Dead*, 3rd ed. (London: Oxford University Press, 1974).

Going to sleep is similar to the bardo of dying [*Chikhai Bardo*], where the elements and thought processes dissolve. . . . Dreaming is akin to the bardo of becoming (*Chönyid Bardo*], the intermediate state where you have a clairvoyant and highly mobile "mental body." In the dream state, too, we have a similar kind of body, the dream body.[11]

An electroencephalograph is an instrument that measures electrical potentials on the scalp and generates records of the electrical activity of the brain; these records are called electroencephalograms or EEGs for short. In 1929, a German scientist, Hans Berger, demonstrated that there were two quite distinct types of EEG patterns: *alpha* (characterized by brain waves cycling 8–13 times per second and *beta* (14–30 cycles per second).[12] Our brains move between alpha and beta patterns depending on what we are doing. Over and beyond that, one part of the brain might be in alpha, while another is in beta. During normal, waking consciousness, our brains move back and forth between beta (when the brain is scurrying around, taking in and processing information from the world), and alpha (where the brain slows down and relaxes, and moves into an idle gear for a while).

Further research revealed two further brain states: *theta* (4–7 cycles per second) and *delta* (.5–3.5 cycles per second). The latter is normally only experienced while deeply asleep and not dreaming. Though dreaming seems to take place during any and all brain states, dreaming is often (but we stress not always) characterized by theta waves.

Though theta waves are slower than alpha, they tend to correspond to a state that is as active in processing inner information as beta is in processing outer information. It is, as if by slowing down the activity of the brain connected with the outer world, the brain is able to get busy with its own inner world. In addition to their presence in the dream state, "theta waves . . .

---

[11] Sogyal Rinpoche, *Tibetan Book of Living and Dying* (New York: HarperCollins, 1992), p. 107.

[12] Marilyn Ferguson, *The Brain Revolution* (New York: Taplinger, 1973), pp. 89–90.

are associated with daydreaming, imagery, and creative visualization."[13] Theta waves are also characteristic of the brain state of advanced Zen meditators. All of these activities are characterized by the *search activity* of the brain. The brain is continually projecting what it expects and sending that information to the rest of the body. When our actual environment no longer corresponds to the brain's expectations, we have to scramble internally to find a new picture of reality that does fit. This might be caused by something life-threatening, such as a sudden confrontation by an enemy. Or perhaps by something as simple as walking into a familiar place (like our workplace) and finding it unfamiliar (perhaps it was unexpectedly remodeled).

Thus dreaming and its daytime cousins tend to be highly active activities often characterized by search behavior. In fact, to the extent that our brains engage in a great deal of search activity during the day, there is evidence that we have less need of dreaming at night.[14] Rinpoche's characterization of "a highly mobile mental body" seems like an excellent metaphor for the

Figure 3. Demon, from a tanka (Tibetan religious painting) depicting the wheel of life, 19th century. (Reprinted from Huber's *Treasury of Fantastic and Mythological Creatures.*)

---

[13] William Murphy, *The Future of the Body* (New York: J. P. Tarcher/Putnam, 1992), p. 359.
[14] V. S. Rotenberg, "REM Sleep and Dreams as Mechanisms of the Recovery of Search Activity," in Alan Moffitt, *et al, The Functions of Dreaming*, pp. 261–292.

nearly constant search behavior going on in the brain. Rinpoche continues with a comparison between the third bardo and its corresponding stage of sleep/dreaming:

> In between the bardo of dying and the bardo of becoming is a very special state . . . the "bardo of dharmata" (*Sidpa Bardo*). This is an experience that occurs to everyone, but there are very few who can even notice it, let alone experience it completely, as it can only be recognized by a trained practitioner. This bardo of dharmata corresponds to the period after falling asleep and before dreams begin. [Or again in the twilight phase just before waking.][15]

Note Rinpoche's emphasis that the "bardo of dharmata" "can only be recognized by a *trained practitioner*" [my emphasis]. This book might be viewed as a guidebook toward creating "trained practitioners of the psyche." Interestingly, dreams themselves show just how far we have progressed in becoming trained practitioners of the psyche. To the extent that we engage with our dreams, consciousness begins to reflect dreams, which reflect consciousness, on and on. Remember the famous "hall of mirrors" scene in Orson Welles' movie "Lady from Shanghai," where it was impossible to decide which image was real and which but a reflection of reality? But, of course, the psyche is much more versatile than a simple physical mirror. Dreams not only reflect, they modify and comment upon the attitudes of consciousness. Consciousness can then review the action of a dream, and even speculate on what a dream has to do with our life. Our task in this book is to learn how to recognize and better participate in that interplay of conscious and unconscious.

From his practical work with the dreams of patients, Jungian analyst and Ericksonian hypnotherapist Ernest Lawrence Rossi has concluded that "self-consciousness is actually a new dimension of awareness that sets the stage for self-reflection and the possibility of changing in a self-directed way."[16] If we

---

[15] Sogyal Rinpoche, *Tibetan Book of Living and Dying*, pp. 107–108.
[16] Ernest Lawrence Rossi, *Dreams and the Growth of Personality*, 2nd ed. (New York: Brunner/Mazel, 1972/1985), p. 13.

engage with our dreams, the dreams reflect that engagement and begin to portray multiple levels of awareness within a single dream scene. Dr. Rossi developed a scale to measure the progressive levels of self-awareness pictured in a dream.[17] Dr. Alan Moffitt, mentioned earlier as demonstrating the ubiquity of dreams during sleep, has used an extended version of Rossi's scale developed by one of his students, Dr. Sheila Purcell, to categorize dreams. Her scale follows:

Self-Reflectiveness Scale

1. Dreamer not in dream; objects unfamiliar; no people present;
2. Dreamer not in dream; familiar people or objects present;
3. Dreamer completely involved in dream drama; no other perspective;
4. Dreamer present predominantly as an observer;
5. Dreamer thinks over an idea or has definite communication with someone;
6. Dreamer undergoes a transformation of body, role, age, emotion, etc.;
7. Dreamer has multiple levels of awareness; simultaneously participates and observes; notices oddities while dreaming; experiences dream within a dream;
8. Dreamer has significant control in, or control over, dream story; can wake up deliberately;
9. Dreamer can consciously reflect on the fact that he/she is dreaming; lucid dreaming.[18]

If this scale seems a little intimidating at first, notice that it begins with no level of awareness at all and proceeds until, at the end, there are many levels of awareness. The authors comment that "[Rossi] sees dreaming and waking as co-determining, co-evolving processes. Both occur spontaneously, but the initial kick that sets this co-evolution in motion is noticing the dream, first from waking, and increasingly from within the dream it-

---

[17] Ernest Lawrence Rossi, *Dreams and the Growth of Personality*, pp. 131–141.
[18] Alan Moffitt, "The Creation of Self in Dreaming and Waking," p. 54. Also in Purcell, Moffitt, and Hoffman, "Waking, Dreaming, and Self-Regulation," p. 212.

self."[19] In their research, they found that the single most effective way for teaching students to increase their level of self-
awareness in dreams was simply to tell them to observe their
dreams and then to try and rate them on the Rossi/Purcell scale;
in addition, they were given a one hour refresher course each
week in the scale. This group was more successful than 1) a
baseline group, who merely recorded their dreams; 2) an *attention
group,* who were trained in detailed dream reporting, but not
told about the scale; or 3) a *hypnosis group,* who, under hypnosis,
were given suggestions for increasing dream recall and increasing consciousness during dreams. The only group that was comparable to the *Rossi Group,* was 4) the *mnemonic group,* who were
taught specific techniques to use both during waking and
dreaming; for example, regularly asking themselves whether
they were sleeping or waking.[20]

So it is possible to learn how to become a "trained practitioner" of dreaming. But let us not confuse technical mastery with
wisdom. Our goal is not to control or even direct dreams (as if
that were possible), but to increase our awareness of, and respect
for, the unconscious forces that go on continuously within us.

HONORING OUR DREAMS

Instead of asking what dreams can do for us, ask how
we may honor the dream.[21]

How would it be, then, if we took our dreaming experience for real, if we accorded it the same respect and recognition we grant our experience while awake?[22]

When we first begin recording our dreams, most of us experience a mixture of awe and confusion: awe at the power and majesty we experience so often in dreams, confusion over the

---

[19]Sheila Purcell, Alan Moffitt, and Robert Hoffman, "Waking, Dreaming, and
Self-Regulation," p. 209.
[20]Alan Moffitt, "The Creation of Self in Dreaming and Waking," pp. 58–60.
[21]Richard A. Russo, *Dreams are Wiser than Men* (Berkeley: North Atlantic Books,
1987), p. 2.
[22]P. Eric Craig, "The Realness of Dreams," in Richard A. Russo, *Dreams are
Wiser than Men,* p. 213.

strange landscape and happenings of the dream world. In an effort to reduce both the awe and the confusion, both of which tend to make us uncomfortable, we may take one of several ill-considered approaches. The easiest, of course, is simply to dismiss dreams as nonsense. This is the answer of many, if not most, scientists. Francis Crick[23] and Graeme Mitchison, for example, have argued that dreams have no meaning whatsoever; they serve only to clean up the psychic garbage of unnecessary memory associations accumulated in the brain during the day.[24] Initially they summarized their position as "we dream in order to forget." Later they pulled back a little from this stark interpretation and said that "we dream to reduce fantasy," or "we dream to reduce obsession."[25] Here is Crick's summary in an unusual scientific memoir he wrote:

> . . . memories are likely to be stored in the mammalian brain in a very different way from the way they are stored in a filing system or in a modern computer. . . . Memories are both "distributed" and to some extent superimposed. Simulations shows that this need not cause a problem unless the system becomes overloaded, in which case it can throw up false memories. Often these are mixtures of stored memories that have something in common. . . . Graeme and I therefore proposed that in REM sleep (sometimes called dream sleep), there is an automatic correction mechanism that acts to reduce this possible confusion of memories. We suggest that this mechanism is the root cause of our dreams.[26]

In a discussion of neural nets in the next chapter, we will see that memories are indeed stored much as Crick describes and, hence, dreams might perform the function of helping clean out

---

[23] Francis Crick and James Watson won the Nobel Prize for their discovery of the double-helix structure of DNA.

[24] Francis Crick and Graeme Mitchison, "The Function of Dream Sleep," *Nature* 312 (1983).

[25] Francis Crick and Graeme Mitchison, "REM Sleep and Neural Nets," *Journal of Mind and Behavior* (1986, no. 7), p. 234.

[26] Francis Crick, *What Mad Pursuit: A Personal View of Scientific Discovery* (New York: Basic Books, 1988), pp. 161–162.

false memories. But it is likely that this is only a secondary function of dreaming. Perhaps the most accepted scientific view of dreaming is that of neurophysiologist J. Allan Hobson, who together with his colleague Robert McCarley, has argued that dreams are an attempt by the brain to bring some order to essentially random neural firing that occurs during REM sleep: "brain-stem neurons activate the brain and generate rapid eye movements, as well as various sensory-motor activities and aspects of the affective system that regulates emotions."[27] Though Hobson feels he has discovered the mechanism that produces dreams, he himself has reverence for the majesty of dreams: "dreaming not only is worthy of participatory enjoyment but has the function of providing us with an opportunity to understand ourselves better. In this view, dreaming is, after all, a message from the gods in the most prophetic sense."[28]

Hobson's research demonstrates that during the night primitive parts of the brain generate random activity from which more evolved parts construct meaningful pattern. From records of dreams, we find that, in creating these patterns, the brain appears able to draw on everything from the current day's experience, to stored personal experience, to knowledge gained indirectly through reading or observation, to knowledge stored in the collective unconscious of the species, even to knowledge that could seemingly only be obtained paranormally.

Among examples of the latter are a number of famous premonitory dreams. For example, in 1945 Winston Churchill dreamed that his life was over. He saw his dead body under a sheet and thought that perhaps this was the end. In fact, it was the end of his great days. The next day he lost the election and had to step down as Prime Minister, a humiliating defeat after his glory days during WWII. Abraham Lincoln dreamed of his actual death days before it happened. He told his wife Mary of a dream in which he saw a coffin in the White House, with soldiers guarding it and mourners weeping. When he asked who had died, he was told that the president was killed by an assassin.

---

[27] J. Allan Hobson, "Dreams and the Brain," in Stanley Krippner, ed., *Dreamtime & Dreamwork: Decoding the Language of the Night* (New York: J. P. Tarcher/Putnam) 1990.
[28] J. Allan Hobson, *The Dreaming Brain* (New York: Basic Books, 1988), pp. 297–298.

I had a premonitory dream that, while not comparing with those of Churchill or Lincoln, presaged an important change in my own life. I dreamed that I received a phone call from William F. Buckley. He told me that he wanted me to write book reviews for his journal. He explained that the current book review editor was Gore Vidal's wife and that she wrote nasty, catty reviews that picked on tiny little points. He hoped that I would have a broader, more positive viewpoint.

Several days later, I received a phone call from a man who was the editor-in-chief of a major Jungian journal. In real life, I knew him only by name and had neither met him, talked to him, nor even had him described to me by others. He is a prodigiously bright man who shares with William F. Buckley the rare trait of speaking so lucidly that it sounds as if everything he says has been elegantly written in advance.[29] He went on to tell me that he had been reading my first book and was very excited. He asked if I would be willing to write book reviews for his journal. He said that the current reviewers tended to pick on tiny little points to the exclusion of the big picture. Altogether an astonishing similarity to the dream that had occurred days earlier! This connection led me not only to a long-time relationship with the editor and his journal, but as an outgrowth of writing for the journal, to eventually write a number of books on Jungian psychology.

Jung had a simple answer to those who regard dreams as meaningless: "No amount of skepticism and criticism has yet enabled me to regard dreams as negligible occurrences. Often enough they appear senseless, but it is obviously we who lack the sense and ingenuity to read the enigmatic message."[30] My own experience is that no one who has actually made an effort to remember and record dreams is able to easily dismiss them; dreams are simply too powerful.

Why we dream might best be left for the reader to decide. But we definitely need to dream. If circumstances deprive us of sleep for an unusual length of time, when we do fall asleep, we tend to drop immediately into dreaming and dream much more

---

[29] As Moliere's M. Jourdain said in "Le Bourgeois Gentilhomme," "Good heavens! For more than forty years I have been speaking prose without knowing it."
[30] C. G. Jung, Collected Works, vol. 16: *The Practice of Psychotherapy*, Bollingen Series XX (Princeton: Princeton University Press, 1954), ¶ 325.

than normally. If we are forced to stay awake for even longer periods of time, we will drop into microdreams that might last less than a second. If we are still not allowed to dream, eventually our behavior becomes psychotic. This is true not only of humans, but of animals as well. All mammals dream,[31] all birds dream, even reptiles seem to have brain states similar to those recorded in higher animals during dreaming. We might speculate that dreams began to appear in the age of the dinosaurs almost a quarter of a billion years ago and were fully developed by 65 million years ago.[32] We all need to dream.

INTERPRETING OUR DREAMS

As in our waking state, real people and things enter our field of vision, so the dream-images enter like another kind of reality in the field of consciousness of the dream-ego. We do not feel as if we are producing the dreams, it is rather that the dreams came to us. They are *not subject to our control but obey their own laws.* . . . In the waking state the psyche is apparently under the control of the conscious will, but in the sleeping state it produces contents that are strange and incomprehensible, as *though they came to us from another world.* [33]

We have now explored and, hopefully, dismissed the idea that dreams are nonsense. Another trap to avoid is forcing the dreams into a "canned" interpretation. For example, there are "dream books" where you simply look up any element of the dream—flying or conflict or gold or whatever—and the book will supposedly tell you exactly what the dream means. Sometimes the dream symbol is even translated directly into numbers that can be used to play the lottery. Instant solution, maybe even instant riches!

This is not to say that such books are total nonsense. They are written and read because most people take dreams more

---

[31] With the exception of the spiny anteater, a very primitive mammal.

[32] We know the latter because opossums dream and they have changed little over the last 65 million years.

[33] C. G. Jung, The Collected Works, vol. 8: "The Psychological Foundations for the Belief in Spirits," ¶ 580.

Figure 4. The storm god Zu in the form of a bird, from an Assyrian cylinder seal, 2340–2180 B.C., roughly the period of Gilgamesh. (Reprinted from Huber's *Treasury of Fantastic and Mythological Creatures.*)

seriously than they are willing to admit. In the absence of information on dream interpretation from "authorities," a folk tradition accumulates. These dream books are predominantly records of folk wisdom concerning dreams. As such, they are filled with about equal parts of profundity and nonsense. As long as dreamers feel free to pick and choose among the interpretations, depending on whether they "click" with their own dreams, these books can be quite useful. The biggest danger is that canned interpretations may prevent dreamers from recognizing that each dream is a miracle filled with riches unique to the dreamer at that particular time and place.

Dream books are ancient. We have records of Sumerian dreams and their interpretations that date back five thousand years.[34] Forty-five hundred years ago, the famed story of the legendary Assyrian hero-king, Gilgamesh, was recorded. Dream pioneer Robert Van de Castle tells us that "in the Gilgamesh saga, dream interpretations which turn out to be correct bring

[34] A. Leo Oppenheim, "The Interpretation of Dreams in the Ancient Near East with a Translation of an Assyrian Dream-Book," in *Transactions of the American Philosophical Society,* 46, Pt. 3, pp. 179–373.

Figure 5. Possible original source for idea of Sphinx? Assyrian winged lion with human head, from the palace of Assurnasirpal 885–860 B.C. (Reprinted from Huber's *Treasury of Fantastic and Mythological Creatures.*)

good fortune, while incorrect interpretations bring misfortune to the dreamer."[35]

Perhaps the most notable ancient dream text is an Egyptian dream book translated and published by Sir Alan H. Gardiner in 1935. The manuscript dates to approximately 1300 B.C., but the material it records is older still, dating to perhaps 2000 B.C., four thousand years ago! This manuscript divides dream symbols into those which are signs of good fortune and those which are bad. For example, a dream of eating excrement is good, and means "consuming his possessions in his house," while if the dreamer drinks warm beer "suffering will come upon him." If a man dreams of copulating with his mother, that is good, and signifies that "men of his province will cleave to him." Copulating with an older woman not his mother, however, was bad and indicates mourning.[36]

[35] Robert L. Van de Castle, *Our Dreaming Mind* (New York: Ballantine, 1994), p. 48.
[36] Joseph Kaster, trans. and ed., *Wings of the Falcon: Life and Thought of Ancient Egypt* (New York: Holt, Rinehart & Winston, 1968), pp. 154–158.

Figure 6. Page from an Egyptian papyrus *Book of the Dead,* which was placed into the tomb with the mummies as a guide for the souls of the departed. (Reprinted from *Lehner's Picture Book of Devils, Demons, and Witchcraft.*)

There is reason behind these seemingly nonsensical Egyptian interpretations. "Many of the interpretations involve a correspondence of ideas and words."[37] Take the dream of a man copulating with his mother, for example. Sexual intercourse is the deepest experience we have of joining with another being. So it is a good way to picture a significant involvement with another person, thing, or idea. A man's mother is the person most

---

[37] Robert L. Van de Castle, *Our Dreaming Mind*, pp. 55–56.

significant to him in childhood. In maturity, this bond gives way to relationships with adult friends. Hence it's not hard to see a dream of a man copulating with his mother as an expression of forming close attachments with others who are significant in his life. As an adult in ancient Egypt, that would then translate into "men of his province" will "cleave to him."

Or take the dream of eating excrement. Scarabs ate excrement and were holy symbols ot the Egyptians! Even today, most dream interpreters might see a dream of eating excrement as positive in the sense that it showed the dreamer was managing to deal with something unpalatable in his or her life; i.e., "getting his shit together." Many of the other interpretations from this ancient text are based on puns which are specific to the Egyptian language of the time; modern dreams still incorporate puns into their vocabulary in much the same way.

Even if we don't consult a dream book, often we use an overly rigid interpretive system that fails to recognize the complexity of dreams. Freud's great contribution to modern dream work was the realization that dreams originate in a part of the brain/mind that predates language, and, hence, necessarily speak in symbols. Unfortunately he was overly reductive in forcing dream symbols to fit his theoretical conclusions about the psyche. For example, in classical Freudian dream interpretation almost every object in a dream was interpreted as a symbol for either a penis or a vagina or a breast, every behavior as a substitute for intercourse.[38] In one massive Freudian textbook of dream analysis (which is otherwise still useful in many ways), symbols for the penis include:[39]

> inanimate objects such as a fountain pen, a pencil, a key, a hat ("an image of power"); persons such as a dwarf, a soldier, a janitor; the common names John, Dick, Henry; and among animals, squirrels, rats, bulls, birds, a cow's udder; . . . fruit such as bananas or pears, plants, the stalks of flowers, trees, roots, trunks ("the

---

[38] I hasten to add that few contemporary Freudians are so reductive.
[39] Emil A. Gutheil, *The Handbook of Dream Analysis* (New York: Washington Square Press, 1970).

latter signifying erection"), geometric figures that are elongated, and the number "3" ("the constituent parts of the male genital").[40]

Obviously, when so many symbols are reduced to so few interpretations, much of the power of a dream is lost. In making any attempt to interpret dreams, it is far better to be willing to let the dream remain a mystery than to try and force it to fit pre-defined patterns. Working with dreams is almost the reverse of panning for gold. Prospectors panning for gold have to pass many pounds of debris through their sieves in order to come up with a fraction of an ounce of gold. In the process they need to be aware that "all that glitters is not gold," and may instead be "fool's gold." In contrast, virtually any dream is inexhaustible; you can return to it over and over, each time finding more gold long after you thought the dream was exhausted. The danger is not so much finding "fool's gold" — even a Freudian interpretation, such as those listed above, usually reveals something true about us — as of simply reveling in the riches we find without making proper use of them. An image that comes to mind is Scrooge McDuck in his vault filled with money and gold and jewels. He rolls in it, dives in it like a porpoise, in utter ecstasy. Yet even a small portion of that gold could be used to transform his life and the lives of those around him.

Once we have recorded a dream so we can return to it later, we need to simply "chew over it." Let our mind (and body — always see if your body reacts to some part of the dream) play with elements of the dream, seeing if meaning begins to emerge. In doing so, it is important to realize that dreams speak in symbols, in metaphors. That's why dream books were compiled; it's useful to read one or two in order to see what others think images in dreams might mean. But that is only the beginning; each of us needs to learn our unique dream vocabularies. We all use the elements of our lives in our dreams — our professions, our hobbies, our friends, our family, TV shows, movies we watch, and so on.

---

[40] Edwin Diamond, *The Science of Dreams*, pp. 47–48.

When psychiatrist Milton Kramer, head of a Cincinnati sleep-disorders center mixed up descriptions of the multiple dreams of ten people, observers were easily able to identify which ones came from the same person, even if the dreams took place on different nights. [Recently deceased] Jungian analyst Edward Whitmont says that such consistency is apparent in dream journals. "The dreams tell a story. It is as if Dream No. 3 knew what No. 15 would be dealing with, and Dream 213 may refer back to something Dream 52 has raised."[41]

Let me give you some examples from my own dream vocabulary. For several years, my wife and I watched reruns of the sitcom "MASH" almost every night. Because this was such a rich show, with a varied and complex set of characters, my dreams often used the characters and setting. When I wasn't present in such a dream, Hawkeye Pierce was often a substitute for me. After all, he was a doctor like me, under pressure like me, and, most importantly, the hero of the show. But I think that virtually all the characters showed up in various dreams, expressing attitudes particular to their characters. At a point when I was preparing to make a major transition in my life, I had the following dream.

Hawkeye and B. J. were leaving a planet on a space ship, and were then going to have many adventures. Another time I dreamed that Hawkeye and the others from the MASH unit were sitting outside at a table celebrating Corporal Klinger's birthday.

On the show, Klinger dressed like a woman, but was obviously masculine. Hence the humor of the situation. Initially he only wore women's clothes in order to try and get kicked out of the army. Gradually, however, he came to appreciate feminine things without losing his masculinity. That was an apt image

---

[41] From "What is the Soul?" in *Life Magazine,* December 1997.

for my situation at a time when I was opening myself up to softer, hidden emotional issues in my life.

Dreams make use of any images we have stored away. If they can find symbols close to consciousness that will do, they make use of them. That's why dreams so often incorporate the events that take place in our daily lives. This has led some dream researchers to speculate that dreams early in the night work through the minutia of the day, in order to resolve problems left over from the day, before moving on to deeper issues. This was one of the assumptions that Crick and Mitchison drew on in constructing their theory that dreams were erasing unnecessary memories from the day. But when a sufficient number of dreams are examined, it begins to appear that even these supposedly mundane dreams are more complex. The dreams pick up the day's people and events as raw symbol material which are then transformed in subtle ways in order to deal with more important issues. I have only seen dreams discuss daily events literally when those events present significant on-going problems that need to be resolved in the psyche.

But dreams aren't limited to our personal knowledge. They can draw on collective knowledge as well. When we dream of a cave, for example, it isn't necessarily there to signify a vagina; though in a particular dream, a cave might very well mean just that, assuming so is too reductive. A cave in a dream not only has all the personal associations we might have to a cave—for example, a trip we took to Carlsbad Caverns—but also the collective memory of what caves meant to our ancestors.

I can recommend an excellent dream book that can help in this respect: the dictionary! Any good dictionary provides not only the definition for a word, but also a mini-history of the roots of the word and often how the meaning of the word changed over time. For almost any word, this etymology can be viewed as the evolution of a symbol. For "cave," my dictionary traces the history of the word back to the Latin *cavus*, meaning hollow. So at its roots, a cave is a hollow, an opening. Perhaps another gateway?

It is also useful to have a number of techniques to use in working with dreams. One approach is to recognize that dreams often have a structure similar to a play. When famed Jungian analyst and thinker Marie-Louise von Franz was asked by an interviewer, "Is there a technique for approaching a dream to discover its meaning?" she replied as follows.

> In Jungian psychology, we have a technique. We compare the dream to a drama and examine it under three structural headings: first, the introduction or exposition—the setting of the dream and the naming of the problem; second, the peripeteia—that would be the ups and downs of the story; and finally, the lysis—the end solution or, perhaps, catastrophe. And if I don't understand a dream, I use that scheme. First I say to myself, "Now, what is the introduction?"[42]

Let's see how this works in practice. We'll start with the setting of a dream. I often have dreams where I'm in some sort of vehicle. If I'm driving my own car, I'm in charge of my own movement in life at the moment. If someone else is driving, I'm not in charge, but merely a passenger waiting to see where I'm going. If I'm on a bus, not only is someone else in charge—doing the driving—but I'm dealing with issues that are collective, not confined to my personal life. When I have some highly unusual vehicle, normally I am trying to develop some new way of moving through life. Here's a dream with an unusual vehicle setting.

> [Famed fictional detective] Nero Wolfe was talking to a man, who asked him if he wasn't going to be making a sharp turn soon. Nero Wolfe answered that he had implicit faith in his French valet. Nero was driving a car, with his valet driving a car ahead of him. They approached a place on the freeway (an actual freeway on which I often drive), where it was necessary to make a sharp right turn in order to get on another freeway. They were stalled for a bit because of a car in front of them. But when they reached the turning point, the valet signaled Nero to turn and they both did turn at just the right point.

---

[42] Frank Boa and Marie-Louise von Franz, *The Way of the Dream: Conversations on Jungian Dream Interpretations with Marie-Louise von Franz* (Boston: Shambhala, 1994), pp. 33–34.

To give some personal background as to why I would have such a dream: I read mysteries for enjoyment; Nero Wolfe is one of my favorite detectives; I've read every book and every story where he's featured. He's a very large man, as I am, but is otherwise very different than me. He's almost entirely a product of his mind, with little regard for feelings, especially feminine emotions. He is extremely lazy and solves all his cases without ever leaving his house. Instead he sends out his assistant Archie to deal with the world, but Archie isn't part of this dream. Nero also has a French chef named Fritz, who sometimes functions as a valet or butler.[43]

So the setting is that Nero, representing a highly intellectual side of my personality, is driving, but the French valet is also driving another car ahead of him. I think most of us would associate Frenchmen with emotion. So, while my intellectual side is in charge of its own destiny, it is smart enough to allow my instincts and emotions to lead the way. This is especially important because it's almost time to make a sharp turn. The dream is probably also using the common pun of a turning-point, a major place of transition. And, in fact, I did successfully make a sharp turn in my life by using my intellect to make some good judgments based on a change in my feelings.

The setting is being in the car, following another car, with the goal of not missing the turn. The middle part — the peripeteia — is simply Nero and the valet continuing to drive along, and being stopped behind another car. The conclusion is a successful one. The turn is made. Thus we have a mini-drama, with a beginning, middle, and an end, all in a concise little package. Of course, not all dreams lend themselves so readily to such an analysis.

Before we close this chapter, I would like to emphasize just how healing dreams can be. A Jungian-oriented therapist, Dr. Harry Wilmer, had many patients suffering from post-traumatic stress syndrome caused by their experiences in Viet Nam. He collected over 350 dreams they had of the war. In contrast with normal dreams, where the people, place, and situations are

---

[43] While Fritz was born in Switzerland, he speaks French and is French in every way.

largely symbolic, these dreams are overwhelmingly simple rep-
etitions of actual horrors experienced in the war. Wilmer said,
"The first thing is to listen, to honor this as an experience, and to
listen with the conviction that this is happening to him for some
psychological reason, and that to get it out of his head, somehow or another, it has to come out to some other human being
who listens without making any great interpretations."

When the experience of the dream had been sufficiently
honored, the dreams would slowly transform and start to become more symbolic. Wilmer termed these new dreams "healing nightmares," as they were still filled with terror, but
reflected an attempt by the psyche to heal the emotional
wounds of the dreamers. This turn toward the symbolic was a
sign that the patient was beginning to get well. The inside was
beginning to be able to come out once again.[44]

Dreams often mirror our state of consciousness. When, like
Wilmer's war veterans, we are stuck in some trauma we can't
escape, dreams cycle endlessly through the same material. Once
we begin to consciously engage with these dreams, a dialogue
begins and the language of the unconscious is symbolic.

---

[44] Stephen Segaller and Merrill Berger, *The Wisdom of the Dream* (Boston:
Shambhala, 1989), pp. 63–67.

C H A P T E R 3

THE BRAIN

*What is inside of you is what is outside of you, . . . what you
see outside of you, you see inside of you.*
—The Thunder, Perfect Mind.[1]

*What is "out there" apparently depends, in a rigorous math-
ematical sense as well as a philosophical one, upon what we
decide "in here."*

—Gary Zukav.[2]

I n chapter 2, we talked of dreams as gateways. The
question, of course, is "gateway to where?" The world
of the dream seems a very different world from the
daytime world in which most of our life takes place. Yet when
we are there, it seems every bit as real. When we wake with the
memory of the dream, is that memory an accurate picture of the
dream world? Or are we already forcing the inside into the
terms of the outside? Let's begin our attempt to answer these
questions with the first outer manifestation of the inner: our
brain.

---

[1] Anonymous, "The Thunder, Perfect Mind," in James M. Robinson, ed., *The
Nag Hammadi Library* (San Francisco: Harper SanFrancisco, 1988), p. 302.
[2] Gary Zukav, *The Dancing Wu Li Masters* (New York: Bantam, 1979), p. 92.

Unless one wished to return to a complete psychophysical dualism, it was best to consider external states as the expression of internal states, which could, moreover, exist independently of this expression.[3]

The first thing we need to appreciate about the brain is that it is really made up of a series of individual brains, each of which evolved at different points in time. Neurophysiologist Paul MacLean's research shows that there are three distinct brains that combine within what we term the "brain." The most ancient, the *reptile brain*, is located at the top of the brain stem, which leads into the spinal cord. Wrapped around it is the *mammal brain*, more properly the limbic system. And wrapped around it is the most recent brain, the neocortex, that almost infinitely wrinkled surface that we normally think of as the *human brain*. Though all three brains necessarily communicate to some extent, in large part they take care of their own business without interference from each other. And that causes some interesting complexities of human behavior.

The *reptile brain*, for example, handles issues of aggression, territoriality, social hierarchies, and ritual. (Note that some rituals predate consciousness. Our task is to construct *conscious rituals*.) Thus, when we get "territorial" over "our" toys, "our" boyfriend or girlfriend, "our" status, "our" scientific discovery, the emotional response wouldn't be out of place in a dog, or a cat, or a bird, or a fish, or even a dinosaur. All react from essentially the same reptile brain, which dates back a quarter of a billion years (to when the first proto-dreams begin to appear, you may recall).

The *mammal brain* "governs social awareness and relationships—belonging, caring, empathy, compassion and group preservation."[4] So, the emotional behaviors we consider to represent humanity at its best are hardly unique to human beings. They appeared a hundred and fifty million years ago, long before human beings appeared on the scene. Given their longer

---

[3] Marc Jeannerod, *The Brain Machine: The Development of Neurophysiological Thought* (Cambridge, MA: Harvard University Press, 1985) , pp. 84–85.
[4] "Gray's Theory Incorporates Earlier Evolutionary Model of 'Triune Brain,'" in *Brain/Mind Bulletin* (March 29, 1982), p. 4.

histories, we would do well to look to other mammals for examples of how we could improve our own behavior in these areas. Wolves, for example, are superb examples for caring, compassionate parenting. When Richard Adams wrote *Watership Down*,[5] I think that many people were surprised about how easy it was to relate to rabbits. While it's true that they were rather anthropomorphized rabbits, there was still a "rabbitness" to them that was both fascinatingly different, yet somehow also recognizably close to human feeling.[6]

Finally at the top of the evolutionary ladder, the neocortex appears: the *human brain*. Though it first emerged in the higher mammals "several tens of millions of years ago . . . its development accelerated greatly a few million years ago when humans

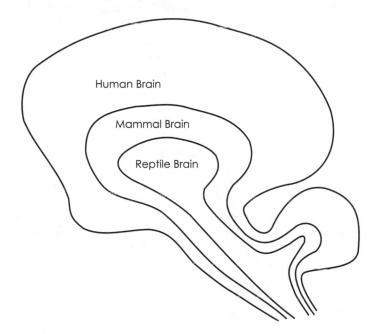

Figure 7. Paul MacLean's Triune Model of the Brain.

[5] Richard Adams, *Watership Down* (New York: MacMillan, 1972).

[6] Adams acknowledged that he had gathered most of his information on rabbit behavior from British naturalist Ronald Lockley's seminal work, *The Private Life of a Rabbit: An Account of the Life History and Social Behavior of the Wild Rabbit* (London: Andre Deutsch, 1965).

emerged."[7] Many neuroscientists believe that a great deal of this brain evolved out of the need to increase visual acuity. The cognitive abilities we treasure so highly appeared as an offshoot of that new visual proficiency. (Though, as we will see later in this chapter, perhaps smell precedes sight in its claim on the increased complexity of the brain.)

The fact that each of these three brains is largely independent of the others helps explain much of our most paradoxical behavior, in which we seem to be at war within ourselves. In his *Maps of the Mind*, Charles Hampden-Turner gives this ironic summary of what the world would be like if MacLean were right (and he is):

> Tradition in this culture might locate precise thoughts in the mind, but vague emotions in the heart, breast, bowels, blood, nerves or viscera (which are indeed controlled by the limbic or mammalian brain). . . . Such a culture might be split between cerebral conceptions of science and the expressive arts, the two barely on speaking terms.[8]

Novelist and Renaissance man C. P. Snow popularized this last split between the scientific and artistic worlds with his famed term "the two cultures."[9] His entire work, especially his series of eleven novels, *Strangers and Brothers*, can be seen in large part as an accurate representation of the interaction between these two views of reality over the course of the 20th century. Though Snow's own view of the possibility of reconciling these inherent conflicts was largely pessimistic, he did see hope in our ability to get beyond individual needs and desires.

> But this isn't all. One looks outside oneself to other lives, to which one is bound by love, affection, loyalty, obligation: each of those lives has the same irremediable components as one's own; but there are also components that one can help, or that can give one help. It is in this tiny extension of the personality, it is in this seizing

---

[7] Carl Sagan, *The Dragons of Eden: Speculations of the Evolution of Human Intelligence* (New York: Ballantine, 1977), p. 58.

[8] Charles Hampden-Turner, *Maps of the Mind* (New York: MacMillan, 1981), p. 82.

[9] See his chapter, "The Two Cultures and the Scientific Revolution"(1959), in C. P. Snow, *Public Affairs* (New York: Charles Scribner's Sons, 1971), pp. 13–46.

on the possibilities of hope, that we become more fully human.[10]

Though these three brains may be in conflict, they also have necessarily learned to cooperate in order to survive and flourish. The coordination between the reptile and mammal brains is, of course, better than their coordination with the neocortex, simply because they have had so much more time to learn to co-exist. Interestingly, MacLean sees our best hope for unifying the three brains in the act of creativity. We have already seen in the previous chapter that creative "search activity" in the brain produces theta waves which spread across the brain as a whole. Accordingly, part of learning to become a "trained practitioner" of the psyche is the ability to tap that creative potential as needed. In that respect, cybernetics and biofeedback expert Elmer Green comments that:

> Our goal is to gain access to what's going on in the lower brain centers, where the deeper levels of consciousness reside. . . . First, though, you have to get the loud noise of waking consciousness turned off, because the information that comes up from the lower brain centers is as delicate and subtle as the draft of a butterfly's wing. The instant you turn too much left cortex attention to it, the information tends to slip away.[11]

We'll talk more of such matters later in the book, but first we need to know more about the brain.

INNATE ANIMAL BEHAVIORS

There was never a king like Solomon
Not since the world began
Yet Solomon talked to a butterfly
As a man would talk to a man.[12]

---

[10] From his chapter called "The Two Cultures: A Second Look," (1963), in C. P. Snow, *Public Affairs*, p. 62. My question is, however, do we become more fully human or more fully animal?

[11] Elmer Green in personal conversation with Tony Schwartz, in Tony Schwartz, *What Really Matters* (New York: Bantam, 1995), p. 188.

[12] Quoted in the preface to Konrad Lorenz, *King Solomon's Ring* (New York: Time Inc., 1952), p. xxi.

As we have seen in the previous section, the brain preserves its evolutionary history in its very structure. It has stored an immense number of behaviors that have proved useful for our ancestors in the human and animal world over vast periods of time. Certain situations repeat over and over for every member of a species. For example, frogs have to be very good at recognizing flies or they will go hungry. Humans have to be good at recognizing faces or they can't function within any human social structure. So there has to be a great deal of specificity in what is stored in the brain.[13] On the other hand, every creature is in large part born into a world unique to it.

For example, though all creatures are born from a mother and, in a majority of species, are raised by the mother, mothers come in a great variety of different packages. Nature has to handle both the specificity and the variety. In his *King Solomon's Ring*, Nobel-prize-winning ethologist Konrad Lorenz explains that "greylag goslings unquestioningly accept the first living being whom they meet as their mother."[14] Lorenz experimented with this "imprinting" behavior and often served as surrogate mother for a variety of little creatures. In the preface, there is a lovely drawing Lorenz did of himself, a friend, and a number of animals. He describes the scene:

> First came a big red dog, looking like an Alaskan Husky, but actually a cross between an Alsatian and a Chow, then two men in bathing trunks carrying a canoe, then ten half-grown greylag goslings, walking with all the dignity characteristic of their kind, then a long row of thirteen tiny cheeping mallard ducklings, scurrying in pursuit, forever afraid of being lost and anxiously striving to keep up with the larger animals. At the end of the procession marched a queer piebald ugly duckling, looking like nothing on earth, but in reality a hybrid of ruddy sheldrake and Egyptian goose. But for the bathing trunks and the moving picture camera slung across the shoulders of the men, you might have thought you were watching a scene out of the garden of Eden.[15]

---

[13] James A. Anderson and Edward Rosenfeld, eds., *Neurocomputing: Foundations of Research* (Cambridge: MIT Press, 1988), p. 2.

[14] Konrad Lorenz, *King Solomon's Ring*, p. 47.

[15] Konrad Lorenz, *King Solomon's Ring*, pp. xxiv–xxv.

The mallards were a triumph for Lorenz, who, for quite a while, hadn't been able to figure out how to make them see him as mother. Through some detective work, he figured out that it wasn't enough to be the first person they saw at birth; in addition, he "must quack like a mother mallard in order to make the little ducks run after me." That turned out to do the trick. Though he looked about as much like a mother mallard "as Calvin Coolidge looks like Metro Goldwyn Mayer's lion" (as James Thurber so perfectly described the wolf masquerading as Red Riding Hood's grandmother in his *Fables for our Time*), "anything that emits the right quack note will be considered as mother."[16]

Nor are such inherited behaviors limited to newborns. Courting rituals are instinctive in many species. An adult male jackdaw fell in love with Lorenz and tried all the wiles that normally proved successful with female jackdaws. For example, he kept trying to feed Lorenz delicacies, like ground-up worms. Like a true scientist, Lorenz suffered this disgusting diet as long as he could. When he was finally so sick of the taste of worms that he refused to open his mouth, the jackdaw filled his ear with worms, then was disappointed when this proved a less than successful romantic strategy.[17]

Figure 8. Courting rituals are also instinctive in many species. (Reprinted from Grafton's *Old-Fashioned Romantic Cuts.*)

A baby's recognition of mother, an adult's repertoire of courting behavior, both innate. Recognition of danger is also often inborn. "Magpies, mallards or robins, prepare at once for flight at their very first sight of a cat, a fox or even a squirrel. They behave in just the same way, whether reared by man or by their own parents." In contrast, jackdaws, who we have seen are born knowing so much about love, have to be taught to recognize danger by their parents. Though they may

---

[16] Konrad Lorenz, *King Solomon's Ring*, p. 48.
[17] Konrad Lorenz, *King Solomon's Ring*, pp. 153–154.

not be born with a sense of self-preservation, they are, however, born with a innate need to protect their young at all costs. Since jackdaws—including baby jackdaws—are black, "any living being that carries a black thing, dangling or fluttering, becomes the object of furious onslaught." Poor Lorenz discovered this to his distress when he accidentally picked up a baby jackdaw and was instantly attacked by the mother. He dropped the baby, and was left with a wounded and bloody hand. Now forewarned, Lorenz systematically explored just how far this instinctual behavior extended. He found, for example, that he could safely carry his black camera, but "the jackdaws would start their rattling cry as soon as I pulled out the black paper strips of the pack film which fluttered to and fro in the breeze." This happened even though the adult birds knew Lorenz to be their friend and no threat to their children. Instinct simply took over.[18]

Though we have considerably more ability to take conscious control of our actions than a jackdaw, a huge amount of our behaviors are already stored away at birth in those reptilian and mammalian brains, ready to be triggered into action when needed.

Figure 9. In some species, recognition of danger is inborn, while in others it has to be taught.

___

[18] Konrad Lorenz, *King Solomon's Ring*, pp. 157–159.

THE DIGITAL COMPUTER
MODEL OF THE BRAIN/MIND

Man seeks to form for himself, in whatever manner is suitable for him, a simplified and lucid image of our world, and so to overcome the world of experience by striving to replace it to some extent by this image.[19]

Throughout history, thinkers have turned to cutting-edge science and technology for new metaphors for thought. This is enormously productive for generating new views of reality, but these metaphors also need to be viewed with some skepticism. In the late 17th century, for example, when Descartes looked for a model of the brain, he turned to hydraulics. Though, to us, this seems an eccentric choice, hydraulics was the most advanced technology of the time, and thus seemed a perfectly reasonable choice to Descartes.

In his model, the pineal gland, which lies behind the middle of the forehead, was "the seat of imagination and common sense." It received information from our senses, then formed an image. So far, if we substituted the brain for the pineal gland, it would sound much like the normal, though outmoded, view of perception still taught in school. But then comes the hydraulics: the pineal gland actually leans toward the "side bearing the image" — which sounds like a Rube Goldberg device — that then opened or closed certain tubes.

Sensory stimulation produced a flux of the animal spirits contained in the heart and arteries. The heart then pushed the spirits into the cerebral cavities, much as the pumps of an organ push air into its pipes. . . . After death the brain collapsed and fluid could no longer circulate.[20]

---

[19] Albert Einstein, "Motiv des Forschens," 1918, in Gerald Holton, *Thematic Origins of Scientific Thought* (Cambridge: Harvard University Press, 1973), pp. 376–377.
[20] Marc Jeannerod, *The Brain Machine: The Development of Neurophysiological Thought* (Cambridge: MA: Harvard University Press, 1985), p. 2.

The most prevalent current cognitive model of the brain/mind views the brain as a complex digital computer, and the mind as nothing more than the programs it runs, which are stored within the structure of the brain. Because of the ubiquity of computers within the fabric of modern society, this model seems totally reasonable to many, but times change and the computer model may someday seem as outdated as Descartes' hydraulic model.

With this disclaimer in mind, let's look at the computer as a metaphor for the brain/mind. The same computer can run many different programs, just as a human can perform many different behaviors. Both the computer and the brain store their programs in some sort of long-term memory until they are needed. In addition to the bread-and-butter programs, the computer needs a special program, normally called an operating system (O/S), which operates at a higher level than any of the other programs. An O/S is like a foreman in a factory who keeps things running smoothly. The O/S knows which programs are running in the computer, which are waiting to run, and which have already run. However, the O/S doesn't decide which programs need to be run, just as the foreman doesn't decide what products a factory should make. This is an executive decision; a human operator tells the computer which programs need to be run in what order of importance. The O/S then schedules the programs, locates them in its long-term memory, runs them when it has the time and resources to do so, prints the results and stores the programs away again for later use. Note that there are at least three levels of operation at work here:

1. The executive level that decides which programs to run;
2. A foreman level which keeps things running smoothly; and
3. A worker level which does the actual work that we associate with the computer.

By analogy, driving a car requires an executive decision on one level of the psyche, the organization and supervision of the necessary behaviors on a second level, and the actual performance of the behaviors on a third level. It is important to realize that only the executive level necessarily involves consciousness. The foreman and worker level can proceed famously without conscious intervention. This latter is an important concept that we can learn from examining this model, even if the model itself proves inadequate.

Just to mention a few diverse examples of the "programs" stored in our brains, we might have stored a program that tells us how to play tennis, another program that enables us to operate a computer much as I am doing now as I write this book. Of course, those high-level programs would in turn be composed of many increasingly smaller programs that range down to the level of directing the appropriate parts of our body to move. All of us have a series of highly complex programs to draw on in social settings. These programs may or may not have anything to do with consciousness. For example, another program might drive our car for us, even if our conscious attention is elsewhere. The wide variety of programs available to a normal person is almost uncountable.

Though the situation is not as clear as with a computer, we also appear to have a higher-level "foreman" function similar to the operating system of a computer, something that keeps track of the total system, loads and runs programs as necessary, allocates resources where needed, etc. Various theorists split at this point, with some arguing against the need for any such central program. It is, however, convenient for our illustration of the digital computer model. Again, consciousness doesn't appear to be involved in this centralized program, any more than it is in the running of any other program. This is not to deny that consciousness can enter the scene and take control of a previously unconscious program; it's just to assert that the psyche is able to operate quite well even in the limited role of a computer, totally devoid of consciousness.

Computer programs are highly organized groups of abstract symbols, specific to the computer within which they are intended to operate. They are stored in some form of relatively permanent memory accessible by the computer, either by being permanently attached to the computer, or by being able to be read into the computer when necessary. The programs of the psyche must be, to some extent, similar. The storage might be something obvious, like a record of synaptic changes in the brain, or less obvious, like a pattern of musculature in the body. Or perhaps some of the programs are not stored in the body at all. Rupert Sheldrake has speculated that the brain operates more like a radio that receives information transmitted from outside itself via radio waves. But the storage need not concern us at this point.

The operating system of the psyche, like the operating system of a computer, necessarily operates at a higher level than the application programs of the psyche. Earlier, I used the analogy of "workers" for the application programs and "foreman" for the operating system, with the "executive" on top making the decisions that the "foreman" organizes and the "workers" carry out. In the psyche, consciousness seemingly forms the highest level of that analogy: the decision maker. If our analogy between computer and human mind can be extended this far, the operating system must also be a program, albeit a highly complex program. In a computer, the most significant parts of the operating system are usually stored in part in a permanent, extremely compact form on one or more computer chips. This makes this part of the operating system incredibly fast at performing necessary repetitive tasks. The remainder of the operating system is stored as software, much like any other program, except that its function is to control the entire computer.

The human equivalent to the part of the operating system stored on permanent computer chips might be the entire structure of the body, with a special emphasis on the DNA structure in the genes, and the nervous system culminating in the human brain. But the entire body structure contributes to the control of itself in ways more complex than any existing computer. However, the analogy is still close enough for our purposes, so we will leave it there for now.

NATURAL SELECTION

> The brain is a selective system more akin in its working to evolution than to computation or information processing.[21]

In our discussion of MacLean's triune model of the brain, we saw that the brain is actually a repository of hundreds of millions of years of evolutionary experience. Konrad Lorenz provided us with examples from the animal world of complex, innate behaviors for mother/child interaction, mating, and rec-

---

[21] Gerald M. Edelman, *Neural Darwinism* (New York: Basic Books, 1987), p. 25.

ognition of danger, among many others. Similar behaviors are, of course, innate in humans, though we have more conscious control over exercising them.

Charles Darwin's theory of evolution by natural selection provides the most commonly accepted explanation for how such behaviors can be innate. Take the adult jackdaw's instinctive attack of anyone grabbing a black, dangling object. Darwin's theory would argue that the jackdaws who were quickest to attack someone who picked up any object even remotely like their children would have more of their children survive. Those jackdaws who were, by nature, slower to recognize potential threats, would have fewer children survive. So the next generation would have more jackdaws who attacked immediately, and so forth.

It's important to contrast Darwin's theory of evolution by natural selection with its predecessor: the theory of evolution by acquired characteristics, which was championed by the great 18th-century French botanist and zoologist Jean Baptiste Lamarck. Lamarck argued that an animal could pass on to its offspring characteristics it was forced to develop because of constraints it experienced in its environment. As a famous example, the giraffe's neck was originally a normal length. As the leaves at the lower levels of a tree were exhausted, giraffes had to stretch to reach the higher leaves. That stretched neck was passed on to the next generation, which in turn stretched further. Eventually the long-necked giraffe emerged.

In contrast, Darwin argued that nothing an animal could do to change itself physically could be passed on to the next generation. Though the original giraffes may have been short-necked, they did undoubtedly vary somewhat in the length of their neck. Because of mutations which occur in any generation of new young (which we now know are a normal part of DNA replication), some giraffes may have especially long or short necks. Those giraffes with longer necks were able to reach more food and were more likely to survive and have children. Of those children, some had longer necks than others and were again more likely to survive and breed. Eventually only those with long necks survived due to the competition with other species who also ate leaves on the lower branches of trees.

As Darwin's theory became almost universally accepted by science, it was natural for late 19th-century theoreticians of the brain to recognize that "the complexity of the behavior of an animal reflects the complexity of its nervous system and thus that evolutionary changes in anatomy can give rise to new behavior patterns."[22] Only recently though has this recognition led to a scientifically sophisticated model of the brain. Nobel-prize-winner Gerald M. Edelman adds a major twist to this understanding with his theory of Neural Darwinism, which goes a long way toward explaining the remarkable ability of the human brain to adapt to a variety of circumstances.

In brief, Edelman looks at the growth and development of an individual brain as a process of natural selection. Because of the evolutionary history of the human brain, it already contains incredible numbers of groups of interconnected neurons. A rough estimate is one *hundred billion neurons*, connected into groups, with each such neuron group including anywhere from 50 to 10,000 neurons connected in highly complex ways. Our genes determine the initial connections of neurons into neuron groups. During the gestation period, the growth and development of the brain of a fetus is accompanied by a selection of perhaps a million such neuron groups. He calls this the *primary repertoire*; in other words, the possibilities that are wired-in at birth. But such hard-wired behavior is hardly sufficient to deal with the variety of the world. As Edelman argues:

> An individual animal endowed with a richly structured brain must also adapt without instruction to a complex environment to form perceptual categories or an internal taxonomy governing its further responses to the world.[23]

Remember Lorenz' contrasting examples of how goslings and mallards decide who is "mother?" Goslings imprint on the first living creature they see at birth, while mallards wait until they hear something that sounds like a mallard's honk. Both are strategies for adapting to the variety of situations they might encounter at birth. Both are built-in genetically.

---

[22] Gerald M. Edelman, *Neural Darwinism*, p. 10.
[23] Gerald M. Edelman, *Neural Darwinism*, pp. 8–9.

But as soon as these innate behaviors have kicked in, experience starts modifying the brain. For example, at birth both eyes of a human baby are connected to all the neurons in the brain's visual cortex. But experience forces each eye to select neural connections for itself, effectively taking them away from the other eye. Since we use both eyes equally, eventually each has about half the pathways, with the resulting neuron groups looking nothing like what they were at birth. If, for some reason, one eye was covered continuously during that developmental stage, the other eye would have all the neural pathways. That would mean that the eye that had been covered could still see the world, but the information would never get to the brain!

In the broad view across taxa, behavior is remarkably diverse and its relation to neural structure appears to be almost capricious. To wiggle the tail of a worm may take a network of thousands of neurons but to flick the tail of a fish only one.[24]

Why is this? Shouldn't evolution gradually make the brain's processes more efficient over time? In fact, most digital computer models of the brain view the programs it stores as logical algorithms, i.e., "a step-by-step problem-solving procedure, especially an established, recursive computational procedure for solving a problem in a finite number of steps."[25] Philosopher of science Larry R. Vandervert provides the most extreme view of this model with his theory of "neurological positivism." He views evolution as refining the algorithms of the brain to ever more perfect functionality, so that the brain, mind, and world form a unity in which it is possible to transform any one into the other through predetermined transformational rules.

This is a lovely model that may in large part be true except for its assumption that evolution keeps honing the algorithms to ever-increasing perfection. The brain doesn't form its programs this way, since in any generation, animals who have to come up with new behaviors to fit new situations draw on the existing structures of the brain, selecting whatever works, then modifying it as is needed.

---

[24] Gerald M. Edelman, *Neural Darwinism*, p. 23.
[25] *American Heritage Talking Dictionary* (New York: The Learning Company, 1997).

The brain is not constructed to think abstractly—it is constructed to ensure survival in the world. It has many of the characteristics of a good engineering solution applied to mental operation: do as good a job as you can, cheaply, and with what you can obtain easily. If this means using ad hoc solutions, with less generality than one might like, so be it. We are living in a particular world, and we are built to work in it and with it.[26]

Another short quote from Edelman brings this all together: "A central assumption of the theory is that perceptual categorization must both precede and accompany learning."[27] We have already built-in many more brain structures than we will ever use. During gestation, we select a healthy-sized group of those structures to draw on in life. After birth we start connecting those together *and modifying them* as we adapt to our environment. The brain grows large and more complex; by the time we reach maturity, the human brain is four times bigger than it was at birth and "no two individual animals are likely to have identical connectivity in corresponding brain regions."[28] Each little gosling is able to follow Lorenz, behaving for all the world knows in identical fashion. Yet each is unique.

We can already see another major problem with the digital computer model of the brain. In digital computers, programs, once written, remain unchanged. Perhaps there is some degradation in the storage and retrieval process, but that invariably makes the program no longer run correctly; it cannot be viewed as analogous to mutations. In contrast, we find in nature, that in many cases a behavior that fits one circumstance can adapt itself to a new circumstance. If the brain is a storehouse of programs, some stored permanently across generations, others only during the course of a person's life, those programs must be something different than the programs stored in a digital computer. Much more like the neuron groups Edelman presents.

Long before we knew much about the actual structure of the brain, psychologist William James already realized that the

---

[26] James Anderson and Edward Rosenfeld, editors, *Neurocomputing: Foundations of Research*, p. 1.

[27] Gerald M. Edelman, *Neural Darwinism*, p. 7.

[28] Gerald M. Edelman, *Neural Darwinism*, p. 5.

brain exists as part of the world, not as a compilation of logical, immutable algorithms.

> *Mental facts cannot properly be studied apart from the physical environment of which they take cognizance* . . . our inner faculties are *adapted* in advance to the features of the world in which we dwell. . . . Mind and world in short have evolved together, and in consequence are something of a mutual fit.[29]

NEURAL NETWORKS

> In the neural network model of the mind, thinking is not following a set of rules but a product of the complex interactions of huge numbers of neurons.[30]

Earlier I mentioned the computer model of the brain, in which things were accomplished hierarchically: an executive decision (by consciousness), was supervised by a foreman level, who in turn had workers accomplish the tasks. The neurological equivalent of the workers are "hard-wired" connections between, for example, different receptors in our eyes and neurons in the brain. Groups of neurons are specialized in order to solve specific tasks — detecting edges, separating various curves, making color discriminations, and so forth. These hard-wired connections are essentially specialized workers who are called into action when we consciously decide to focus our attention somewhere. They are the parts of the brain most like digital computer programs.

Most of these hard-wired connections are directly coded by DNA sequences in our genes. There are living organisms simple enough that every single neural connection is described genetically. But for most animals, and certainly for human beings, our genes hardly begin the task of making such connections. For example, we have already said that at birth both eyes of a baby are connected to all of the neurons in the visual cortex of the brain.

---

[29] William James, *Psychology (Brief Course)* (New York: Holt, 1890), pp. 3–4.
[30] William F. Allman, *Apprentices of Wonder: Inside the Neural Network Revolution* (New York: Bantam, 1989), p. 22.

Then experience intensifies some connections and eliminates others, until each eye has about half the connections. This is more efficient than having to describe all those connections genetically. So we end up with specialized workers in the brain, specialized workers who didn't have to be fully described genetically. This method of "writing programs" is similar to how simple programs, often referred to as "macros," are created within word-processing, spreadsheet, or database programs. Basically, you notify the computer to begin recording a macro, you perform a series of tasks, then turn off the recording when you're done. The resulting macro program is stored and available for later use.

But much more of the brain's solutions to problems don't involve such hard-wiring at all. Nor do they involve the hierarchical, logical solutions of the digital computer model. Instead "best-fit" solutions are created in a way that seems like heresy to those who believe in a strictly cognitive model of the brain. "Computers are typically given a list of instructions to follow. A neural network, on the other hand, is "taught" through a series of examples."[31] This new way of viewing the brain has been termed the *neural network* model.

A good metaphor for how this model works is a small town meeting. Imagine that everyone in town has gathered in the town hall to discuss some problem that concerns everyone to a greater or lesser extent. Let's say they are considering changing the zoning laws so some land previously zoned for residence only is now going to be opened up to commercial interests. Since this is a small town, everyone in the room has some connection to everyone else, but the strength of those connections may vary considerably. For example, some people may be relatives, others friends, others acquaintances, still others business colleagues. At the start of the session, some people will probably already have definite feelings one way or the other about the issue. For example, the proposition will undoubtedly have been presented by businessmen who want to make use of this land. They will already have made connections with others to try and win them over to their point of view. In contrast, those with homes near the area under

---

[31] William F. Allman, *Apprentices of Wonder*, p. 12.

discussion may be strongly opposed to having it opened up for commercial use. They will probably have already talked this over with some friends as well.

So, as the meeting begins, some people already have strong feelings for and against the proposition. But it's likely that most people won't yet have formed an opinion. When the meeting begins, the two opposing sides present their cases. As they do, those who were initially indifferent to the issue begin to lean one way or the other. They may do this on the basis of the issues or on the basis of their personal or business connections with someone on either side of the issue. Remember that the strength of the connections between the townspeople will vary considerably. As the discussion continues, there will be rising and ebbing tides as one side or the other gains temporary ascendence. Gradually the discussion will begin to die down as everyone eventually comes to a decision. A consensus will emerge and the new zoning will either be accepted or turned down.

When the group leaves the meeting, not only is the issue resolved, but the strength of their connections with each other may have changed during the session, not only on this issue but in general. Some members of the group may realize that they really should spend more time with some person who impressed them. Or they may have formed an antipathy for another person simply on the basis of what that person said or how he or she behaved in the meeting. No one can predict in advance exactly who would end up for and against the proposal and how strongly they would feel about it. The final outcome is a unique solution to the original problem, one that would be impossible to logically dissect.

This "town meeting" model is a close approximation to how the brain solves problems. Just imagine that the neurons in the brain are the townspeople, and the strength of the connections between various neurons varies, just as the townspeople vary in their feelings of attachment to each other. At any point in time, when some new solution needs to be created by the brain, the neurons are in various stages of activation, just as the townspeople were at the start of the meeting. As impulses flow between the various connections, some neurons turn on and others turn off, depending on the strength of the signal received, and certain particulars we can ignore in this discussion. Eventually,

Figure 10. A good model for how the neural network model works is a small town meeting. Imagine that everyone in the town has gathered in the town hall to discuss some problem that concerns everyone to greater or lessor extent. (Reprinted from Harter's *Men: A Pictorial Archive from Nineteenth-Century Sources.*)

a new stability arises which leads to a resolution of the original issue, whether it was pattern recognition or a need for action.

In 1982, John Hopfield, a physicist at Cal Tech, proved mathematically that a network of simplified neurons acting in this way can process information and solve problems.[32] Algorithms weren't needed. Hierarchies weren't needed. The brain can make use of the neuron groups it already has present in order to form new connections and arrive at a generalized solution.

---

[32] J. J. Hopfield, "Neural networks and physical systems with emergent collective computational abilities," *Proceedings of the National Academy of Sciences* 79 (1982), pp. 2554-2558, reprinted in James A. Anderson and Edward Rosenfeld, *Neurocomputing: Foundations of Research*, pp. 460–464.

In order to model how this actually works in practice, neuroscientist Gary Lynch collaborated with computer scientist Richard Granger in developing a computer model of a 500-neuron network to see if it could learn to discriminate between different smells. They had two different smell groups: "cheese" and "flower," with variations of each. At first the neural net came up with a unique pattern for each smell, but eventually, after it was exposed to the individual odors more times, the neural net produced one pattern for the cheeses and another for the flowers. Without any instruction or any logic, it was able to generalize the group to which they belonged from specific examples. If they exposed it to any of the "cheese" smells, for example, it would always identify "cheese."

But something even more startling happened: as they continued to give it more sniffs of each particular cheese, at some point, the general pattern disappeared and the neural net produced specific patterns within the general pattern for the various cheeses. Now the network could not only discriminate "cheeses" from "flowers," but also different varieties of "cheeses." Granger said that:

> We're thrilled with it. With the first sniff, it recognizes the overall pattern and says, "It's a cheese." With the next sniffs, it distinguishes the pattern and says, "It's Jarlsberg."[33]

The model that discriminates different smells is a perfect example of a neural net, as the neuron groups formed are essentially random and unpredictable in advance. If the same model were wiped clean of its memory, then retrained, it would again learn to discriminate the smells, but it would do so with a totally different set of connections in the network. Lynch says "Smell isn't spatial or temporal. It doesn't exist in a dimensional world. It's like pure thought."[34] We will return to this idea later.

This is especially interesting because mammals were the first animals to develop a keen sense of smell. Developing a keen sense of smell may have been what made the mammalian

---

[33] William F. Allman, *Apprentices of Wonder*, p. 76.
[34] William F. Allman, *Apprentices of Wonder*, p. 77.

brain, then later the primate brain (the cortex), first grow in size. Lynch theorizes that when the dinosaurs disappeared, the mammals needed better vision as well as better smell. That produced a different type of neural connection. For example, the brain deals with vision with a combination of digital computer solution and neural net solution. Some areas of vision work like directly wired algorithmic problem solvers, with specific neurons for specific tasks. Other parts work like smell, with no particular wiring necessary. And, in fact, we can train computer versions of neural nets to perform complex visual tasks, such as detecting varieties of curves, much better than the same task can be done by direct connections of particular neurons to particular parts of the brain.[35]

Of course, for neural networks to be more than just a model, it's necessary to prove that the brain actually can and does modify itself. It appears that action is the critical element in changing the brain's structure. This was originally recognized by psychologist/philosopher William James, who in this area as in so many others, was prescient. James said that "no mental modification ever occurs which is not accompanied or followed by a bodily change. . . . Our psychology must therefore take account not only of the conditions antecedent to mental states, but of their resultant consequences as well."[36]

More recently, R. Held proposed that every physical movement leaves a trace in memory. When the same movement is executed again, it combines with the original trace and the combination is saved in memory. When they are slightly different, the movement program would be modified to take this difference into account. In the words of French neurophysiologist Marc Jeannerod, "action is thus the means of verifying whether a hypothesis conforms to reality.[37]

From 1959–1974, Held conducted a long series of experiments to test this. When our senses are systematically distorted, by a lens that inverts our vision, for example, we gradually adjust to this until we see perfectly normally again.

---

[35] William F. Allman, *Apprentices of Wonder*, pp. 76–77.

[36] William James, *The Principles of Psychology*, vol. 1, Dover unabridged reprint. (New York: Henry Holt, 1890; reprint: New York: Dover, 1950), p. 5.

[37] Marc Jeannerod, *The Brain Machine: The Development of Neurophysiological Thought*, p. 132.

But this only happens if we are able to move and test *our* inner view of reality.[38] Of course the action can be internal as well as external.

Let's call these neural net solutions "natural programs," to distinguish them from "algorithmic programs" such as the digital computer model of the brain requires. Natural programs have practical advantages over algorithmic programs and nature always likes to improve its odds of success. Because natural programs are stored in an overall pattern, the more times the pattern is accessed from various input situations, the stronger it becomes. Because it is a pattern spread across a wide number of neurons, even if a substantial portion of the neurons are damaged or destroyed, the pattern can usually still be reproduced from those that remain. If the newly reproduced pattern is less than perfect, it will get better again as it is reused.

Before we leave this section, it is important to emphasize that the neural net solutions of the brain take place between the receptors and the neocortex, the *human brain*. The connections to, from, and largely within the mammalian and reptilian brains are directly wired.

FROM TRIUNE BRAIN TO HOLOGRAPHIC UNIVERSE

Let's take stock of what we've already discovered about the brain and see to what extent it begins to point toward the unitary world we promised in the introduction, the world in which knowledge emerges from the inside out. First, we found that we possess not one brain but three, each representing a different stage of evolutionary history and each largely dealing with operations specific to itself. Though we think of ourselves largely as rational beings who make conscious decisions about our lives, a great deal of our behavior is already stored at birth in the older reptilian and mammalian brains. We looked at some examples from ethologist Konrad Lorenz of how the mother/ child relationship, courting behaviors and recognition of danger

---

[38] See Marc Jeannerod, *The Brain Machine: The Development of Neurophysiological Thought,* pp. 133–137.

are built-in for several different species of birds. But quite obviously, such behaviors are also built-in for dogs and cats and monkeys—and humans. Though the development of the neocortex allows us to exercise much more control over those inherited actions than, for example, Lorenz' jackdaws, who attack anything that is black and moves in a certain way, we would do well to realize just how much of our actions are determined directly by those more primitive brains within us. Then the human brain comes along after the fact and thinks up supposedly rational reasons why we were driven by irrational behaviors.

Then we saw how evolution operates within the structure of these three brains. Each brain, especially the two oldest, can be regarded as a repository of solutions to problems once presented to species that preceded humans, and later adapted by humans. We've seen that the brain's structure tends to be composed of "good enough" solutions to problems. Where a species needs some special ability specific to itself, such as a frog's need to quickly spot moving bugs, or a human being's need to recognize a wide variety of faces, a new brain structure forms gradually due to evolutionary pressure. But otherwise, if something worked for a lizard that later evolved into a bird, there is no need for the structure to change. If something specific in the bird's environment requires a change in its behavior, the change is likely to be a modification of the original solution rather than something radically new, developed specifically for birds.

Further, there is no evolutionary need for even out-of-date neural structures to disappear, unless they conflict with necessary structures. Doesn't Jung's concept of archetypal structures begin to seem a little less strange, given how the brain has developed? Let's take an example: I think most of us would accept that falling in love must have some such archetypal structure. After all, it happens in very similar ways for all humans in all cultures. In that respect we aren't much different than the jackdaw who fell in love with Lorenz and tried to feed him worms. Human cultures have a wide variety of ways in which courtship behavior is expressed, so we know that the specific behaviors are not hard-wired, as they are for the jackdaw. But the similarities of behavior are more striking than the cultural differences, or for that matter, even the species differences.

With the increased development of the visual centers of the neocortex, those "good enough" behavioral structures undoubtedly began to form neural linkages with visual structures to provide images that matched to those behaviors, so that archetypes developed two faces: image and behavior. So archetypes are a reasonable way to describe the way the brain appears to be structured.

Within limits, the digital computer model of the brain is a fair start at an approximation to the way these hard-wired archetypal structures are stored and function. Just as a computer can load special purpose programs as needed, the brain can call upon special purpose "programs" when it needs them. Some of these programs are written by evolution and stored in the brain's structure at birth; some are learned in the course of our development. These learned but still directly-wired programs are probably best exemplified by the connections between some of the receptors in the eyes and the neurons in the visual centers of the brain.

But we also saw that with the increased development of the neocortex in humans (and the higher primates), a second type of brain structure appeared, which can best be represented by neural nets. Rather than a hard-wired solution, the brain gradually comes to a solution which is spread widely over the brain's structure (and here, by brain, we are largely talking of the "human brain," the neocortex). We presented a "town hall" model of how this process might operate. Later in the book, when we discuss chaos theory, we will present this theme again in terms of "attractors."

Even more than the hard-wired solutions created by evolution, these "natural programs" (as we termed them), are "just-so" stories. There is no logical necessity for a particular structure to emerge as a solution to a problem, since the solution is spread widely over the structure of the brain, and many other possibilities would do just as well.

The neural net model also offers a possibility for the *unus mundus*, the unitary world, to extend past the storage within a single human being. Clearly this method of solving problems and storing memories over an entire structure does the job, or nature would never have developed it. At this point, we don't know exactly how it operates, except that it is global rather than local.

Neurophysiologist Karl Pribram was the first to notice that this ability of the brain to store solutions and memories over its entire structure is similar to a hologram, in which a three-dimensional picture may be stored by interference patterns on film. He believes that there are two storage structures going on simultaneously in the brain, one more localized (defined through connections between neurons), and another global (through the astonishingly numerous dendritic connections within the brain). We will address his theory at length later, but what is important now is that he thinks that the holographic brain is, itself, a part of a holographic universe. Just as the brain is able to store and access information over its total structure, the universe is able to store and access information over every part of itself, including each human being. In that respect, Pribram has this to say:

> It isn't that the world of appearances is wrong; it isn't that there aren't objects out there, at one level of reality. It's that if you penetrate through and look at the universe with a holographic system, you arrive at a different view, a different reality. And that other reality can explain things that have hitherto remained inexplicable scientifically: paranormal phenomena, synchronicities, the apparently meaningful coincidence of events.[39]

Synchronicity, the "apparently meaningful coincidence of events," as Pribram puts it, is the topic of our next chapter.

---

[39] "Holographic Memory: Karl Pribram Interviewed by Daniel Goleman," in *Psychology Today* (12, no. 9, Feb. 1979), p. 72.

SYNCHRONICITY

Nature uses only the longest threads to weave her patterns, so each small piece of her fabric reveals the organization of the entire tapestry.

—Richard Feynmann.[1]

W e have already seen how dreams can be gateways into the inner world. Sometimes the gateways open up when we're wide awake. Let me start with some personal examples.

I began my training as a clinical psychologist at a "halfway home." It was intended to serve as a temporary support structure for severely disturbed young adults before they could move out on their own. Those who demonstrated their ability to function relatively independently could move into small apartments within a few miles of the main facility. The main facility had a prior existence as a two-story Southern California motel, complete with a now seldom-used swimming pool. A central dining room had been added, together with offices for staff and TI's (therapeutic interns, such as I was).

---

[1] Nobel-Prize winning physicist Richard Feynmann in *The Character of Physical Law* (Cambridge: MIT Press, 1965), p. 34.

Though the halfway home was located on a large street, it was relatively quiet and isolated by a tall concrete wall that ran entirely along the street side. Other walls enclosed the other limits of the facility. I don't want to make it sound like a prison, as the setting was quite friendly, given the limits of a facility with a relatively small area. You entered through an open doorway cut into the wall on the street, took a right, then a left, and you were suddenly inside this strange setting. After I had been there for a while and gotten my feet wet, so to speak, I found that as soon as I entered the doorway, before I could see into the facility, I would know if things were "crazy" that day or stable. There was one other therapist, a young woman, who had the same ability to sense the level of craziness. If I felt a certain queasy feeling as I walked in, I would immediately check with her. She would either confirm that bad things were already happening or, if not, that she felt the same way and was waiting for something to break. And it would—I don't recall our ever being wrong.

Now how did we know that? Though it is difficult to express, I felt that the craziness struggling to come out of the patients actually passed inside me. I'm not sure whether the environment was an intermediary carrier or not; I think it was. But there were no environmental clues for me to note; rather I felt something inside myself—a "queasiness" as I characterized it earlier, which I translated into things being crazy outside. Sometimes we both said that things "smelled" crazy, which is a common reference to an intuitive feeling.[2] In any case, the key fact is that I had found a gateway that could open, even when I was conscious. I experimented further with it.

---

[2] There is actually research that rats can distinguish a difference in smell between schizophrenics and non-schizophrenics. See Edward T. Hall, *The Hidden Dimension* (Garden City, NY: Anchor, 1969), p. 49. Rats have a more developed sense of smell than humans, but there is speculation that intuition is an outgrowth of smell. Jung felt that thinking, feeling, and intuition were all outgrowths of sensory perception. Intuition would be a natural outgrowth of smell, thinking out of sight, feeling out of hearing and speech. In my clinical work, I've found that the two main varieties of "craziness" seem to be further outgrowths of a normal predisposition to one or another of these functions. Thinkers become schizophrenic, feelers become manic-depressives.

In an altered state of consciousness we use a different
metaphysical system. If we really use a different metaphysical system (and not just think or talk about it), we
are in an altered state of consciousness. These two
phrases are different ways of describing the same thing.[3]

I started using altered states of consciousness in working with
the patients, without any real knowledge of what I was doing—
except that it helped. By altered states, I'm not implying anything that most would regard as mystical: if the patients were
anxious, I would match my breathing and movements to theirs.
When we were in synchrony (which we will discuss later), I
would gradually slow my movements and breathing, and so
would they. Usually patients would end up in something like a
trance state. At that point, if I opened myself to them—there's
no other way to express it—I would find their emotions flowing
through me as if they were my own. I would cry their tears, or
express their anger. Sometimes, I would have pictures in my
mind that weren't from my own life memories. Usually I would
find out later that these images were from patients' lives. Often
the images were symbolic rather than literal. From doing dream
work, I was used to translating such images.

Of course, I wasn't always so wise when I experienced feelings that weren't my own. One patient, nicknamed "Red," was
extremely paranoid. For some reason, he developed a fixation
on me. He would come around the office where the other TI's
worked and say nice things about me to the other members of
the staff, usually making sure I could hear him. I didn't realize
what was going on, as Red wasn't one of my patients, and I
didn't know him very well. In retrospect, I realized he was developing an intense fear of me, and was trying to win my favor
by placating me.

I was pleasant enough to Red since he meant nothing special to me. But his anxiety around me increased. Since this was
all coming out of him rather than being an objectively accurate
response to a frightening situation, there was probably little, if
anything, I could have done to defuse his anxiety. Then one

---

[3] Lawrence LeShan, *The Medium, the Mystic, and the Physicist* (New York, Viking
Press, 1974), p. 155.

night, when I was outside talking with another patient, Red started shrieking his anger and fear at me from his room. The basic litany was that he knew I was out to get him, but he'd get me first. And he had a knife!

That's a frightening situation! I discussed it the next day in a supervision group with other TI's. They were supportive, but I did not experience any relief. I became anxious whenever I saw Red, though he now avoided me as much as he had previously sought me out. Soon I was anxious anytime I was at the halfway home, whether Red was around or not; everyone began to seem dangerous. I began dreading my visits. I even considered terminating my residency there (as so many other TI's had already done).

Then one day, it hit me that I was experiencing paranoia, just as Red experienced paranoia. I hadn't recognized the symptoms. With no category in which I could put this nameless anxiety I was experiencing, it infiltrated insidiously into my whole outlook on life. As soon as I realized I was experiencing paranoia, the paranoia ceased. The same day, Red had an acute psychotic episode, where he ended up curled in a fetal position and had to be taken to a hospital for short-term treatment. As far as I can determine, Red never even saw me that day. When he returned to the facility several days later, I was a proper therapist again, trying to find some way to help a patient in pain. He and I had no further problems.

Another time, the patient helped me, rather than me helping the patient. I was experiencing an emotional problem, and was in a good deal of pain. I was stretched between two sides of a moral dilemma and wasn't willing to change my self-definition. I helped myself deal with my pain in the way I usually did at that time: by helping patients deal with their pain. I was having a session with a patient, who I'll call Jean here. Jean had a very, very hard time articulating. Every word was a struggle because she was constantly experiencing so much emotion — usually anger — that the emotion intervened between her thought and her speech. I had never heard her able to speak clearly about anything.

Suddenly, out of nowhere, her speech became startlingly clear, and she told me exactly what I needed to do to resolve my emotional problem. It was like the best therapist/guide in the world was there, who had been listening carefully to my problem, and now gave me exactly the counsel I needed. Of course, I hadn't even mentioned my problem to Jean. As quickly as it happened, Jean was back to her old speech pattern, discussing her issues. Remember the quiet voice from within that we discussed a number of times in the chapter on dreams? This was the same sort of voice, one that had to be honored. The difference now was that the voice wasn't coming from within me in a dream, or even from within me in a waking state, but from outside me, from the mouth of my patient. And, afterward, Jean knew nothing of what had happened.

SYNCHRONY, INTIMACY, AND PSI

This two-step process—first the pattern, then the explanation—is how we try to reduce the power of chance over our lives. All intelligence, at however low a level, tends to take the first step. . . . It's usually said that Science consists of this two-step process, plus a third step which consists of adding fresh bits to the pattern and seeing whether the explanation still works. But in fact quite a lot of science never gets further than the first step.[4]

Psychologist and dream pioneer Henry Reed, whose wonderful first dream we have already discussed, has in recent years done similarly pioneering work in psychic connections between people—extra-sensory perception. He proposes something that sounds strange only because we think of ESP as strange: that ESP is an extension of normal intimacy between people. Think about that. When we are with a stranger, most of our communication is limited to the content of the words we speak. As in all interchanges between two humans, there is also an unspoken body language that we read unconsciously, but when we don't know someone well, there are definite limits to our ability to interpret the other's actions.

Then imagine two lovers in the early thrall of their love, where they are so intent on each other that the rest of their environment virtually fades from their awareness. They notice

---

[4] Peter Dickinson, *Chance, Luck and Destiny* (Boston: Little, Brown, 1976), pp. 30–31.

Figure 11. Imagine two lovers in the early thrall of their love, where they are so intent on each other that the rest of their environment virtually fades from their awareness. (Reprinted from Grafton's *Humorous Victorian Spot Illustrations.*)

anything and everything about their loved one: every movement, every glance is significant to them. If we watch them closely, their actions are like a wonderful dance, part choreographed in advance by the archetype invoked by love (much like Lorenz' jackdaw) and part unique to their pairing. They rarely miss a step in this elaborate dance.

Then think of a long-married husband and wife with a good marriage. Notice just how few words go on there. They understand each other so intimately that each can virtually complete the other's thoughts. They no longer need the intensity of attention of the two young lovers since the other is so embedded within them that they are able easily to function either separately as individuals, or as a pair, each complementing the other to form a whole that is neither one nor the other.

In the field of emotion, which is a phenomenon very much on the border between physiological and psychological reality, rhythm is essential. In states of strong emotion we make rhythmical movements (stamping our feet, for instance) and tend to repeat endlessly the same thoughts and utterances. This led Jung to suspect that unconscious complexes might have a periodical rhythmic nature.[5]

Research by experimental psychologists William Condon and Ray Birdwhistell and by linguistic anthropologist Edward T. Hall demonstrated that this synchronous dance of individuals is more than a metaphor. Filming human interactions in a variety of situations, then viewing them at slowed-down speeds, they were able to watch how tiny, nearly imperceptible body movements by one person cued movements by another. Hall comments that: "viewing movies in very slow motion, looking for synchrony, one realizes that what we know as dance is really a slowed-down, stylized version of what human beings do whenever they interact."[6] This ability to synchronize our movements to our environment "appears to be innate, being well established by the second day of life, and may be present as early as the first hour after birth."[7]

Earlier in this chapter I told how I would consciously synchronize my movements and breathing to that of patients in distress, then guide them into an altered state. In a remarkable example of how this can operate at an unconscious level within a full group, one of Hall's students filmed school children playing in a playground during lunchtime. Though at the first viewing of the film, the children seemed to be each "doing their own thing," after repeated viewing, Hall and his student noticed that one little girl was especially active. During the course of the lunch break, her play took her over the entire schoolyard. The movements of all the other children came in synchrony with her own as she moved into their territory, until the whole group was moving in an unconscious symphony, led by the little girl as conductor. When Hall and his student asked an expert on rock music to watch the film, he was actually able to find a currently popular tune that fit the rhythm so perfectly that once it

---

[5] Marie-Louise von Franz, *Time: Rhythm and Repose* (New York: Thames and Hudson, 1978), p. 22.
[6] Edward T. Hall, *Beyond Culture* (Garden City, NY: Anchor, 1977), p. 72.
[7] Edward T. Hall, *Beyond Culture*, p. 73.

Figure 12. The whole group was moving in an unconscious symphony, led by the little girl as conductor. (Reprinted for *Dore's Spot Illustrations.*)

was "synchronized with the children's play . . . [it] remained in sync for the entire 4½ minutes of the film clip."[8]

Dr. Reed's work starts with this synchrony, then moves beyond into psi. He is a frequent lecturer and workshop leader who uses these occasions to conduct group experiments that benefit both the audience and scientific research. For example, he plays "The Getting to Know You Game" with these audiences. He has a number of varieties of this experiment. In one, a member of the audience, the "agent," reads a nursery rhyme or the alphabet or, more recently, simply counts backward from 50 to 1. The audience is asked to both concentrate on the voice and observe anything going on within themselves as they listen. Afterward, they share what went on inside them. "Purely subjective responses show surprising relevance to the objective facts concerning the vocalist's personal life, beyond matters of temperament and mood to facts in the vocalist's environment."[9]

---

[8] Edward T. Hall, *Beyond Culture*, p. 77.
[9] Henry Reed, "Intimacy and Psi: A Initial Explorations," *Journal for the American Society for Psychical Research*, October 1994, 88, p. 88.

This technique maximizes the information that Dr. Reed can receive and validate. More recently, he has developed several one-on-one variations which maximize the number of people who can be helped by the intuitive insight. In each, he has the audience break into pairs. One variation proceeds as above, with one person counting slowly backward from 50 to 1, while the other person notices his own stream-of-consciousness. Afterward, the receiver tells the speaker what he experienced, and the speaker tells what does and does not fit his life.

In the "problem response" version, the speaker picks an issue on which she would like to receive advice, but keeps it secret during the countdown. Dr. Reed has found that the listener's response usually provides insight into the problem. Finally, in a "soul retrieval" mode, the listener is:

> given a format for a story to imagine while traveling on the river of sound of the speaker's voice: go underground, meet an animal helper, find the lost soul fragment of the speaker, heal it and return with it, learning from it what it can contribute to the speaker's life. At the end of the countdown, the listener shares the story with the speaker and gets feedback. This procedure, as simple as it is, with untrained people, strangers as partners, has proven very profound, healing, [calling up] powerful emotional reactions.[10]

I remember participating in a similar experiment at a workshop in Asilomar in 1981, led by a medical doctor and clinical psychologist. He concentrated on a particular variety of psi: psychometry — the ability to access information about a person, by physical contact with the person or with an object belonging to the person. He felt that psychometry was a normal ability that anyone could use, one which was especially useful for therapists. Because this was a controversial stance, he came up with a hilarious cover term for the use of psychometry for psychological diagnosis: "holographic diagnostic techniques." We each paired up with someone else from the group whom we had never met before. Then we took turns as "sender" and "receiver." The receiver would hold

---

[10] Private communication from Dr. Henry Reed.

the sender's hand and concentrate on his or her own inner process. As a receiver, I remember that I got a picture of a farm house and an old couple. It turned out that the person I was paired with had, in fact, been raised on a farm by his grandparents!

This was so impressive to me that, when working with patients, I always took note of whatever images came up in my own mind, remaining open to the possibility that it had something to do with my patient. This works equally well in everyday life. I think that we all do this a great deal of the time, reading information about the other person on an unconscious level, then acting on it ourselves with no intervening conscious thought. The process of observing our inner process while engaging in normal interactions with another person seems awkward at first, but becomes almost unconscious after a while (if this isn't a contradiction in terms).

SYNCHRONICITY

It is the nature of synchronicity to have meaning and, in particular, to be associated with a profound activation of energy deep within the psyche. It is as if the formation of patterns within the unconscious mind is accompanied by physical patterns in the outer world. In particular, as psychic patterns are on the point of reaching consciousness then synchronicities reach their peak; moreover, they generally disappear as the individual becomes consciously aware of a new alignment of forces within his or her personality.[11]

Often we find that gateways open in our lives in ways that don't fit readily into traditional views of reality. Jung coined the term *synchronicity* for meaningful coincidences, occurrences that had significance for us, but for which there is no simple causal explanation. We are all familiar with such events, yet we tend to dismiss them as coincidences, ignoring the fact that it is their meaning for us that seems to trigger them in our lives. For example, while thinking of someone the phone rings and it is that

---

[11] F. David Peat, *Synchronicity: The Bridge Between Matter and Mind* (New York: Bantam, 1987), p. 27.

same person on the phone! Or needing a special piece of information and a book arrives in the mail with just the information that is needed. Consider a small synchronicity that occurred while working on this chapter. A fan of a previous book, with whom I had no contact for a year, suddenly wrote to ask if I could tell her what synchronicity was. Clearly, her interest in synchronicity wasn't what made me write about it, nor was my writing the cause of her interest. The two were separate, yet came together in a way that was meaningful for both of us. How can we explain this (other than, of course, to ignore the fact that it had meaning for both of us and to dismiss it as coincidence)?

In my own life and in the lives of those around me, I have repeatedly found that synchronicities increase in intensity, frequency, and clarity at special times. These include times of transition, ceremony, crisis, fear, and other exceptional times: birth, death, marriage, separation, changes in professional life, etc. Accordingly, when synchronicities begin to appear in my life, I know that something special is afoot, and I try to get in touch with those synchronicities, to become more centered, more aware of what the psyche is trying to tell me. When I'm successful with this process, the synchronicities increase in frequency. Psychologist Ira Progoff agrees with this position. He says:

> By definition one cannot *cause* synchronistic events, but on the basis of observations in this area over the last twenty years, it does seem to me to be possible to develop in a person an increased sensitivity to synchronistic events, and especially a capacity to harmonize one's life with such occurrences.[12]

When I was still seeing patients in a clinical setting, I found that nearly all my patients went through similar issues at the same time. This was especially noticeable at watershed points in their lives. For example, when after a lot of progress, my first patient of the day was stuck on what could be loosely termed a father issue (or a mother issue or a variety of others), I knew that I

---

[12] Ira Progoff, *Jung, Synchronicity, and Human Destiny* (New York: Dell, 1973), p. 132.

would be dealing with the same issue throughout the day with most of my patients. This was most marked when, after being stuck for a long time, one patient suddenly had a breakthrough. It was quite exciting to see a whole series of epiphanies throughout the day. But a similarity of theme that lasted over an extended period of time was the more common synchronicity that I noted. Since I saw patients who varied from very disturbed patients at a halfway home to outpatients in a counseling center, the particulars of the issue would take different form. But then all Jungians are used to seeing the variety of clothes that a symbol wears. Victor Mansfield said in his recent book on synchronicity:

> An important implication of acausal connection through meaning is that in *synchronicity the meaning is primary while the objective and subjective events that correlate are secondary and contingent.*[13]

After I had noticed this was going on, I went out of my way to remove any possibility that these events were actually causal and that perhaps I was the cause. I would simply note what was going on with the first patient, then stay a bit more detached than otherwise in the early part of a session, so that I wouldn't be feeding the patients cues as to what I expected. In retrospect, I think this was a needless precaution on my part, since usually they would come in with the issue plainly on the table. And, of course, it wasn't only my patients that were going through those issues at the same time; so was I. This recognition that what was happening in others might say something to me, and vice versa, was one of the most helpful tools I ever discovered in dealing with this strange unitary world we live in.

Again notice that this required me to discover a previously hidden meaning; that a patient's issues were not only theirs, but mine as well. That in turn caused me to focus more closely on the cycles of emotions and events that we all pass through, either observing others in order to learn more about myself, or observing myself in order to learn more about the situation others

---

[13] Victor Mansfield, *Synchronicity, Science and Soul-Making* (Chicago: Open Court, 1995), p. 26.

were in. There was already a meaning there trying to come out, but it required focus on my part to see it.

As time went on, I began to notice that these synchronicities extended to those with whom I was connected closely in any way, not only those I saw routinely in my daily life, but also those from whom I was separated by distance and only communicated with occasionally. Often very specific types of events would show up across the board. Here I often found that one or another of us might be a few days or even a few weeks behind or ahead of the main group of people, but that seemed only to make this more believable. Synchronicity isn't necessarily simultaneity in time, but simultaneity in inner experience. Time and again, this awareness has enabled me to help people who wasn't forthcoming with their situation, but who I knew needed help because they were going through something similar to myself and other friends.

> Jung's definition has led to frequent misunderstandings because "coincidence in time" is generally understood as an astronomical simultaneity dependent on clock time. It is rather, a *relative simultaneity*, to be understood as the subjective experience of an inner image coinciding with an outer event. Only in this experience is the time difference abolished, since the event, whether in the past or future, is immediately present. It may happen that inner image and outer event are connected together by an objective, clock-time simultaneity, but that is not the decisive factor. The decisive factor lies in a subjectively experienced, relative simultaneity.[14]

I've also found that synchronicity extends to the inanimate objects that are most significant in my life, especially my car and my computer. Undoubtedly this is an extension of the process I've already been presenting: a pattern emerges in the psyche and bursts forth in some way that grabs my attention and causes me to further focus. So it picks not only the people who are significant in my life, but the objects. I've grown so used to

---

[14] Aniela Jaffé, *From the Life and Work of C. G. Jung,* R. F. C. Hull and Murray Stien, trans. (Einsiedeln, Switzerland: Daimon Verlag, 1989), p. 20.

this happening that I'm no longer startled by it. I just stop and look at the event as if it were a dream and interpret it that way. For example, on the few occasions when my car has overheated, it coincided with my pushing myself too hard and not realizing it. My battery never dies when I've got lots of personal energy, only when I'm drifting into depression.

Though I've had many similar experiences with my computer, I remember one event in particular. Several people, connected with Subud,[15] who had read one of my books contacted me, and asked to see me informally. I was working at my computer and had forgotten just when they were going to arrive. Suddenly my computer went crazy, with all sorts of strange symbols racing up and down the computer screen. Nothing I could do would change it, including turning off the computer and rebooting. Just then the doorbell rang to announce my visitors, so I left the computer as it was and went down to meet with them. Their visit turned out to be a very strange and memorable event, though one that ended up having more effect on the life of another friend of mine that it did on my own. When they left, I returned to my computer, which had returned to normal and which has never again duplicated this strange behavior.[16]

Psychologists Allan Combs and Mark Holland see these physical instances of synchronicity as serving the purpose of enlightening the psyche to something it is overlooking.

> One of the authors likes to refer to such coincidences as "perverse synchronicity." The key is to relax into the moment, realize that life will not end if the next stop light turns red, and try to be centered on yourself. Doing this can lead to surprising results. You may find, for instance, that the tricks are actually not so bad. Upon

---

[15] Subud is an estoric group founded by a Javanese mystic named Bapak Muhammed Subuh. Subuh discovered an inner force, an energy, which could be transmitted to others through a group practice called the *latihan* (the Indonesian word for "exercise").

[16] For those who think that this might sound like an incipient computer virus, it took place on a little Commodore 64 before destructive hackers bothered with personal computers. The only other time a similar event happened was on another Commodore 64 when lightning struck the wiring of our house. Unfortunately, that computer was permanently damaged.

regaining your composure, you often discover that each trick is followed in time by another coincidence that provides a solution to it.[17]

Jung agreed that when the energy in the unconscious was powerful enough, synchronicity could extend to inanimate objects:

> It often seems that even inanimate objects co-operate with the unconscious in the arrangement of symbolic patterns. There are numerous well-authenticated stories of clocks stopping at the moment of their owner's death. . . . Other common examples are those of a mirror that breaks, or a picture that falls, when a death occurs; or minor but unexplained breakages in a house where someone is passing through an emotional crisis.[18]

In his spiritual autobiography, *Memories, Dreams, Reflections*, he gave a personal example. He had been arguing with Freud about these inexplicable, seemingly paranormal events. Just as Freud was leaving, Jung felt a burning sensation in his diaphragm, as if it were a "glowing vault." At that moment, there was a sharp sound from the bookcase, and both turned to it, fearful that it might fall. "There," Jung said to Freud, "that is an example of a so-called catalytic exteriorization phenomenon." When Freud pooh-poohed this as nonsense, Jung told him he was mistaken and said, "to prove my point I now predict that in a moment there will be another such loud report." And, of course there was.[19]

This story illustrates the difficulty in finding handy little intellectual boxes in which we can put such events. Did Jung cause the event because he was so heated up by the discussion, so irritated at Freud, that it burst out of him? Then the second time, he actually consciously caused it to happen? Perhaps. Or

---

[17] Allan Combs and Mark Holland, *Synchronicity: Science, Myth, and the Trickster* (New York: Paragon House, 1990), p. 107.

[18] C. G. Jung, "Approaching the Unconscious" in *Man and His Symbols* (New York: Anchor Books, Doubleday, 1964), p. 55.

[19] C. G. Jung, *Memories, Dreams, Reflections* (New York: Pantheon, 1973), pp. 155–156.

perhaps, as Jungian analyst Aniela Jaffé suggests, since "Jung was in a highly emotional state . . . his consciousness was drawn, so to speak, into the realm of the unconscious and he was able to 'know' the coming event."[20] How about my patient who turned briefly into my counselor—did my need for help cause her to speak? Perhaps, or perhaps we're in deeper waters than simple causal explanations, even those that involve paranormal causality.

Aniela Jaffé points toward one answer: "One of the main points of Jung's investigations on parapsychology is that *synchronistic events are manifestations of an archetype.* In other words: the archetype is their 'organizer.'"[21]

Notice how similar this is to our relationship to our dreams. We can neither control nor organize our dreams, that organization has to come from within. Though we can't control our dreams, we can become more attuned to them. Even lucid dreams are more like a dialogue with the unconscious than a drama that we are writing from scratch. The process of learning to listen to the psyche is similar, whether we are listening to our dreams or observing the synchronicities that occur in life. In that process, something new emerges inside. At this stage, it is an archetypal pattern, unformed in any way we can appreciate. It then clothes itself in the images, emotions, and behavior we have experienced in our life, as well as those we have learned of second-hand through art, entertainment, and education.

First the pattern forms. As it emerges it catches our attention, so that we listen—we *focus.* My experience leads me to be believe that perhaps focus is the necessary catalyst for synchronicity to occur. Transitional times take us out of the mundane "robot" existence we normally lead and cause us to focus on our life. Once we notice a synchronicity and open ourselves to the possibility of other synchronicities, we become ever more focused. A good metaphor for the process might be that synchronicity serves as a lens that concentrates the diffuse world of the unconscious until it emerges into consciousness. When a visual lens focuses diffuse light, the light becomes more

---

[20] Aniela Jaffé, *Apparitions and Precognition* (New Hyde Park, NY: University Books, 1963), p. 191.
[21] Aniela Jaffé, *Apparitions and Precognition,* p. 192.

and more intense. Focused enough, it can actually cause combustion. The focus that synchronicities bring into our lives is similar, though here the combustion creates *not* flames, but *meaning*.[22]

Is it difficult to imagine how archetypes can organize our inner world and outer events? Jung's answer, which I mention in the introduction, is that archetypes are *psychoid*—both physical and psychical. This is a strange way of viewing things that tends to turn our normal view of reality, even paranormal reality, on its head. For example, think about Dr. Reed's "The Getting to Know You Game." I presented it as if there was a speaker, or agent, and one or more receivers to make it simple. But we can also view the same situation as if an archetype of relationship is being awakened and because of its psychoid nature, the entire environment—including all the people—are acausally connected in a meaningful event. This is most pronounced in the "soul retrieval" version mentioned earlier, in which a consciously chosen archetypal fairy-tale structure is used as the organizational principle. Because this outer format closely matches what is actually going on in the experiment, it is especially powerful for the participants.

SALIENCY

> When we try to understand nature, we should look at the phenomena as if they were *messages* to be understood. Except that each message appears to be random until we establish a code to read it. This code takes the form of an abstraction, that is, we choose to ignore certain things as irrelevant and we thus partially select the content of the message by a free choice. These irrelevant signals form the "background noise," which will limit the accuracy of our message.[23]

---

[22] This idea that focus creates meaning is, by the way, basically the same theme that Colin Wilson explores throughout most of his books, though he doesn't address synchronicity per se.

[23] J. M. Jauch, *Are Quanta Real?* (Bloomington: Indiana University Press, 1973), p. 64.

Jung conceived of synchronicity as an explanatory principle to deal with meaningful acausality. Unfortunately, it is this very acausality that causes traditional science to dismiss synchronicity out of hand, no matter how many examples are presented. Classically, science has been based on physical cause-and-effect. Relativity demonstrated the equivalence of matter and energy, which somewhat diluted the picture. Quantum mechanics brought probability into the equation so that, at the quantum level, we could no longer speak of direct cause-and-effect, simply of probabilities of outcomes. More recently still, a new factor — information — has moved into a central position. Mathematician, psychiatrist, and experimental psychologist William Sulis has proposed that naturally occurring complex systems are information driven. Since almost everything in nature of much interest is a complex system, information moves to the forefront and Sulis proposes an alternative to physical or energetic causality, which he terms *saliency*. "The critical issue is not whether information is present, for that will always be the case, but rather whether or not the information which is present is salient for the system in contact with it."[24] In other words, the environment might be filled with information, but the information is only useful when its complement is found.

Even random noise can be seen as filled with information for an organism that needs something to complement itself. In other words, saliency is neither in the organism nor in the environment, but only in the coming together of both. For example, remember that dreams seem to be produced by random neural firing that especially affects the emotional parts of the brain (the limbic system which we termed the mammal brain). The neocortex, the human brain, jumps into action, trying to make sense of the biologically meaningless information flooding the brain. It structures the material into story lines — dreams — which address unresolved issues, attempt to integrate new experience, and project possibilities.

Saliency provides a scientifically rigorous alternative to causality. Notice that not only have we moved past the concept of mechanical or energetic causality, we are now dealing with a to-

---

[24] William F. Sulis, unpublished paper for UNESCO conference, 1999.

tal pattern that includes both what would formerly have been viewed as the cause and the effect. Both are now part of a single pattern in which the information in one links with the information in the other in order for something new to emerge. What is that link? I would suggest it is "meaning," though Sulis, like any good pure scientist, objects to finding meaning in nature. Commenting further about synchronicity and saliency, however, he comes very close to the position we are taking in this book when he says that, "I like to think of reality like a giant ocean, and synchronicity like the currents. There are many differing currents. Some are local, some are global. One can form endless patterns but some are mere random fluctuations, while others are significant. Not knowing the currents can get one killed. Knowing the currents one can travel far. Not everywhere mind you. And not always in the way planned or desired. It is knowing when to go with the flow, and when to cross the flow."[25]

We can see examples of saliency occurring at many different levels broadly throughout nature, from the subatomic level upward. At the behavioral level, remember how Lorenz' baby goslings and mallards seemed to "imprint" a "mother archetype" onto Lorenz? For those who feel uncomfortable with Jung's term *archetypes* in the context of animal behavior, elsewhere I've coined the alternate term *cognitive invariants,* "a somewhat ungainly term that might be more welcome and intelligible to modern science. Cognition is the mental process of knowing or perceiving, invariant means constant; hence those constants which in part determine our knowledge of reality."[26] So, we could say that the babies drew on a cognitive invariant for the child's experience of the relationship between mother and child.

Key is that these examples, and the others that Lorenz provided, of mating behavior and defensive behavior are inborn hard-wired predispositions that are triggered by highly specific information cues from the environment. An image of lock and key comes to mind. Imagine these cognitive invariants as wholly contained behaviors (with accompanying predisposi-

---

[25] William. F. Sulis, private email correspondence of 5/11/99.
[26] Robin Robertson, *Beginner's Guide to Jungian Psychology* (York Beach, ME: Nicolas-Hays, 1992), p. 39.

tions toward images) which are locked until a highly specific key appears in the environment to open the lock and release the behavior. Note that this is not either physically or energetically causal; information is all that is exchanged. And neither the mother nor the child causes the experience of the mother/child relationship to be activated; rather both together form this new whole. If the imprinting has occurred as it should onto a mother gosling or mallard, the other side of the relationship would have also been triggered. In Sulis' words: "Saliency does not depend upon the energy which is exchanged but rather upon the form, texture, and context within which the exchange takes place. Pattern takes precedence over substance."[27]

Jung viewed synchronicity as a subset of acausal events in general, one in which meaning was central, psychological meaning. But saliency allows us to stretch the concept of meaning down to a point where it no longer has to be psychological meaning. Saliency can occur without synchronicity but synchronicity cannot occur without saliency. Sulis and the author both agree that synchronicity in an extended sense pervades reality; that is, there are many more acausally linked events happening at any point in time than causal events. And even causal events are better viewed within the broader view of saliency and multivariance.

Saliency provides a way to approach synchrony, and from synchrony to synchronicity. Imagine a room full of pendulum clocks, initially all at rest. Then, one at a time, start each pendulum moving. If you're careful, at first you may be able to have all of them at different parts of the cycle of their swing. For example, one might be just starting its downward swing, one may have reached the bottom of its swing, ready to move up again, a third might have reached the peak of its swing, ready to move backward once more. If you leave them alone for a while, then come back, you may be surprised to find that now they all swing together in perfect harmony. The movement of each has had an effect on each of the others. Gradually they come to a single rhythm that harmonizes all the movements before.

---

[27] William F. Sulis, unpublished paper for UNESCO conference, 1999.

In physical systems, this mutual feedback of *salient* information is termed *entrainment*. It operates in biological systems as well as in physical systems. For example, that's why crickets chirp together rather than at random, why groups of fireflies tend to flash at the same time. There have been experiments that show when women are living together isolated from others, their menstrual cycles come into balance in the same way. Or reconsider the lovely example we gave earlier in our discussion of synchrony, of the little girl who led everyone in the school yard into her rhythmic movement. We could say that the girl's movement caused each of the other children in turn to match her rhythm, but it's more elegant to think of the rhythm already being there and that gradually the whole playground matched the rhythm. The little girl was the first to tap into the rhythm, and part of that movement included her moving all around the playground. If the rhythm had been strong enough, it might well have pervaded the playground even if the little girl didn't move throughout the whole playground.

Whether we term it saliency or meaning, the universe is filled with information. My own opinion is that meaning pervades the universe at every level, and we barely tap that source of limitless meaning. That meaning lies behind our personal destinies as much as it defines the movements of stars in the sky. We have only to find the right keys for the locks that open the gateways.

THE CHAKRAS

Chakras are psychic centers in the body that are active at all times, whether we are conscious of them or not. Energy moves through the chakras to produce different psychic states. Modern biological science explains this as the chemical changes produced by the endocrine glands, ductless glands whose secretions mix into the body's bloodstream directly and instantaneously.

—Harish Johari[1]

We have already seen how evolution has preserved the development of consciousness in the very structure of our brains. In this chapter, we will see that our evolutionary history is preserved at an even more primitive level in a series of *psychoid* (to use Jung's term) structures that have been noted and recorded by virtually every culture throughout history. Though these structures appear to be truly psychoid—that is, body and psyche—their locations in the body correspond to the major glands of the body. The glands, in turn, are able to send messages throughout the entire body, including the brain. The connection between these structures and the world beyond the body seems to be through the process of breathing, but not

---

[1] Harish Johari, *Chakras: Energy Centers of Transformation* (Rochester, VT: Destiny Books, 1987), p. 1.

simply physical breathing. Cultures which have discovered these structures argue that when we breathe, we are bringing in air and also an energy that is omnipresent throughout the universe. This basic energy is transformed in the body into a life energy, then further transformed by these psychoid structures into forms specific to our basic life needs. Now this may well be a metaphor rather than what actually happens, but since this entire model is ignored by Western science, we are not yet in a position to judge. We will come at it from several different directions in this chapter in an attempt to demonstrate that it is, nevertheless, worthy of our consideration.

THE BREATH OF LIFE

> This repeated filling and emptying of breath is the rhythm of the universe itself, sending waves to strike at the root-impulses of Kundalini. When Kundalini is struck, she awakens, uncoils and begins to rise upwards like a fiery serpent, breaking upon each chakra as she ascends, until the Sakti merges with the Siva in deep union, samadhi or enstasis.[2]

Many ancient traditions believe that the body contains a life energy that concentrates at key parts of the body, each of which correspond to a specific level of human development. The Egyptians taught that there were thirty-six "subtle arteries" called *metu,* which transport this energy to various parts of the body where it collects. The ancient Chinese had this energy entering the body through the crown of the head and moving to three energy centers located in the brow, heart, and lower body. Tibetan Buddhism expanded the three centers to five: the brain, throat, heart, solar plexus, and sexual organs. The Hindu philosophy has the system most known to the outer world, with *chakras* of energy located above the crown of the head, at the brow, throat, heart, solar plexus, spleen area above the sex organs, and the perineum at the base of the body, between the anus and the sex organs.[3]

---

[2] Ajit Mookerjee, *Kundalini: The Arousal of Inner Energy* (Rochester, VT: Destiny Books, 1982), p. 24.

[3] Benjamin Walker, *The Encyclopedia of the Occult, the Esoteric, and the Supernatural* (New York: Scarborough, Stein & Day, 1980), pp. 218–222.

The Greeks were aware of a similar set of centers, probably from the Egyptians. Their knowledge, in turn, was passed on in Gnostic and later alchemical tradition. Similarly, Kabbalist tradition, Sufi tradition, and many African traditions from one end of the continent to the other, all have such centers of concentration of energy. The system that I learned from half-Irish, half-Cherokee medicine worker Harley Swiftdeer was adapted from several Native American systems, especially those of the Hopi and Maya. It has a system of energy centers called *wheels* (and sometimes *worlds*) identical in location and general function to the Hindu chakras.

This energy system has been ignored in the Western scientific world, largely because the energy that drives this system—called *pneuma* in Greek, *prana* in Sanskrit, *ch'i* or *qi* in Chinese, *ki* in Japanese, *lung* in Tibetan, *ruah* in Hebrew, *ruh* in Arabic, and *mana* by the Polynesians and Hawaiians—does not correspond to any energy Western science believes to exist.[4] In recent years, there has been a slight increase in openness to this tradition, at least to the extent of the medical community allowing acupuncture, which is based on this energy system, to be used as an adjunct to traditional methods for anesthesia and pain relief.

The word *chakra* from the Hindu tradition, means "wheel" in Sanskrit, just as the Hopi/Maya word did. These traditions use the word *wheel* because they view these energy centers as constantly turning, constantly in a state of flux, at right angles to the spine, much like wheels on an axle. Of course, this picture of a turning wheel is only an analogy to the idea of energy constantly increasing and decreasing in three (or more) dimensions. But it's a useful analogy. We might view the chakras as a series of interlocked wheels or gears, each turning constantly, each connected to the turning of wheels both above and below itself, forming a unified system throughout the body. If any wheel stops turning properly, it affects the harmony of the entire system.[5]

Most of us have been taught to look contemptuously on so-called spiritual healers. We watch fundamentalist preachers who heal "with the power of Jesus" by laying on of hands, and

---

[4] Benjamin Walker, *The Encyclopedia of the Occult, the Esoteric, and the Supernatural*, pp. 222–223.
[5] I'm indebted to Harley Swiftdeer for this metaphor.

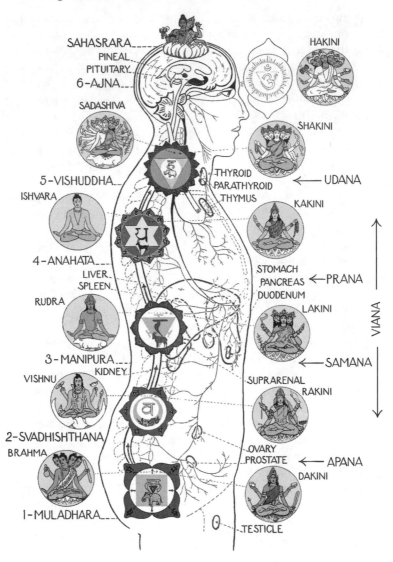

Figure 13. The Hindu chakras and Kundalini Paths. (Reprinted from chart issued by Samuel Weiser. Used by permission.)

laugh at the credulity of the people who believe in such unscientific nonsense. Yet we probably also feel somewhat uneasy about the cures we see effected; we ask ourselves if they are all really phony? We prefer not to have to think about such issues. Yet the tradition of healing with energy is an ancient one. And it's not very difficult to experience the same force yourself.

Start with someone who is willing to have you attempt to feel his or her chakras without laughing or making jokes at your expense. The process is subtle enough that discouragement can ruin it. It is possible to feel your own chakras, but it's easier to feel someone else's.

Shake your hands vigorously while you move your arms up and down. Rub your hands together, then cup an imaginary ball of energy between your two palms until you can feel the ball of energy, ignoring whether it exists anywhere other than in your mind. Move your hands closer and then farther apart, feeling the energy contract and expand like a rubber ball. Then cup your hands loosely and move them up the body of your helper. Don't touch his or her body, just keep your hands six to eight inches away. Be receptive to sensation in either or both hands, or between the two hands. You may feel heat, or cold, or tingling, or something less easily describable. A personal method I use, which I haven't found elsewhere in the literature on chakras, is to hold one hand out from the body, loosely cupped and parallel to the floor. Now run the other hand over the helper's body (remembering not to touch it) and see if you can't feel something in the cupped hand. For me, I can make a more subtle judgment of the position and energy of the chakras this way than merely feeling with one or the other hand.

This experience is subtle, and the ability to feel it comes and goes at first, but if you persevere, you should actually feel the chakra energy. And you will find that they exist where the ancient systems say that they exist. If you find other centers, less pronounced, you will discover that there is a literature that also pinpoints those smaller centers as well. For example, you should be able to feel energy around the joints of the body.

Doctor and alternative healer Brugh Joy says that 99 percent of the people he introduces to hand scanning (his term for feeling chakra energy) can feel chakras. Even discounting that Brugh Joy attracts sensitive and intuitive people to his seminars, probably most people, including you, can feel chakras, if they are open to the concept.

With the experience of feeling chakras to make this less academic, let's look at the connection between energy and breath from another angle. Traditionally the energy that flows through the body is viewed as connected with our breathing; sometimes it is literally called "the breath of life." But it isn't the physical breath that is being referred to; it is a more subtle force that enters and leaves the body with our respiration. This is breath as energy, as pneuma, prana, or ch'i.

As we will see for ourselves in the next chapter on meditation, breathing stands at the junction between those functions that we consciously control and those controlled by our autonomic nervous system. In other words, it is under the control of both the *sympathetic* and *para-sympathetic* systems of the body. Our body will automatically breathe if left to itself, but we can take conscious control over breathing and vary it if we like. Biofeedback training, for example, can be used to learn how to gain conscious control of breathing and other normally automatic functions, such as heartbeat and skin temperature. Breathing, however, remains the most important function that we all regularly control!

Linkage between the sympathetic and para-sympathetic systems of the body is regulated by the hypothalamus, a brain organ largely located in the *reptile brain,* but which controls the *limbic system* (the mammal brain). Deep meditation, which we will discuss at length in the following chapter, can bring about a state where breathing nearly stops. At that point, since breathing forms a junction between these two systems, the hypothalamus brings both to a stop and all mental impulses cease. This creates the moment of oneness or spiritual union known under so many names in so many cultures.[6]

The hypothalamus in turn is closely connected with the pituitary gland, the master conductor of the glandular action of the body. At the point when the hypothalamus (in conjunction

---

[6] Katsuki Sekida, *Zen Training* (New York: John Winterhill, 1975), pp. 47–52.

with the thalamus; we're simplifying things here) brings the nervous system to a halt, the pituitary gland sends messages to all the glands of the body, which in turn send messages to the entire body, bringing it into a state of non-being.[7]

Now, hardly surprisingly, we find that if we examine the locations of the glands, they are closely connected with the chakras, each chakra corresponding to one of the major glands. The esoteric traditions insist that none of these actions are the primary reason for the functioning of this energy, however. Their picture is that this energy is drawn in through the crown chakra at the top of the head, into a series of chambers of the brain called ventricles. There the energy takes the form of a "heavenly dew" called *ros*. It is ros that travels down through the body until it arrives at the base of the spine and awakens the basic energy force: the *Kundalini*.[8]

Before we turn to the Kundalini itself, let us examine this rather complicated series of actions again. Most major esoteric traditions visualize the life force as being drawn into the body through the crown of the head. That energy is translated into a form useable by the body. The body has developed a system of glands and connections between the sympathetic and parasympathetic systems that correspond to the locations of the energy systems in these secret traditions. Through observation of, and sometimes control of, our breathing, we can regulate the limbic brain system, the hypothalamus, the pituitary gland, the other major glands, and from there the entire body.

Most of the traditions I've cited as identifying energy centers similar to the chakras also have methods for awakening those energy centers. "Awakenings," means developing energy centers to the point where they function more fully; they function to some extent whether awakened or not.[9] Since energy is transformed depending on its container, the Kundalini is experienced differently, depending on which chakra is awakened. At a key point in my own personal development, I had a dream that said that the 5th, 6th, and 7th chakras had just opened up.

---

[7] Steven Rose, *The Conscious Brain*, pp. 273–277, 332–336.

[8] See Benjamin Walker, *The Encyclopedia of the Occult, the Esoteric, and the Supernatural*.

[9] For more information, see Gopi Krishna, *Kundalini: The Evolutionary Energy in Man* (Boston: Shambhala, 1971).

WHEELS OF ENERGY/WORLDS OF CONSCIOUSNESS

> Man is created perfect in the image of his Creator. Then
> after "closing the door," "falling from grace" into the
> uninhibited expression of his own human will, he be-
> gins his slow climb back upward. Within him are sev-
> eral psychophysical centers. At each successive stage of
> his evolution one of these comes into predominant play.
> Also for each stage there is created a world body in the
> same order of development as his own body, for him to
> become manifest with.[10]

Here I am going to stray from the Hindu names and descriptions of the chakras, and use the Native American version that I
learned from Harley Swiftdeer. In this system, the chakras were
called *wheels* because they are energy centers that can actually
be physically experienced. But each wheel also corresponds to a
level of development, both of individual consciousness and of
the universe. As the latter, the chakras can be seen as "worlds"
of consciousness.

The first chakra, the "Creation Wheel," corresponds to the
boundless energy of the sun. It is the wheel of creation and especially of procreation. That is why it is experienced so often
through sexuality, why Freud could think that it was the primal
energy itself. But it's not; it is only the lowest level manifestation of that energy. It is located at the base of the spine. When
you are sitting properly, it would point straight up from the
ground into your spine. In some traditions, it's located between
the ovaries for women, making it the only sexually differenti-
ated chakra. The Creation Wheel is concerned with basic, primal
energy, as yet unformed; hence it is awakened when we need to
deal with actual survival or basic life needs. At a more general
level, at this stage, you have to deal with giving form to unfo-
cused energy, unformed new possibilities.

The chakras — as worlds — also correspond to the development of the entire universe. All parts of the universe are seen as
containing the history of the universe's development up to and
including themselves. Here we encounter again the concept of

---

[10] Frank Waters, *The Book of the Hopi* (New York: Viking Press, 1963), p. 26.

the unitary universe, the *unus mundus,* in which the microcosm and the macrocosm, the inside and the outside are one. At this universal level, the Creation Wheel represents the first concentration of matter and energy in the stellar systems, and before that, if the Big Bang is correct, in the primal explosion itself. This is the first point in evolution where any concentration, any order is apparent. More basic even than this state would be that of chaos, of non-differentiation, a state prior to the chakras.

Second is the "Path Wheel" (also called the "Crystal Wheel"), located between your genital area and your navel. At the universal level, this chakra marks the stage at which the stellar systems cooled further and planetary systems formed. Here energy is trapped into rigid, angled structures like a crystal. This chakra is concerned with choice and power (especially willpower). Having experienced the primal energy through sexuality, if we don't fall prey to the many problems presented by sexuality, that energy becomes available to us as willpower that we can use to direct our actions. The most common problems are rigidity and abuse of power.

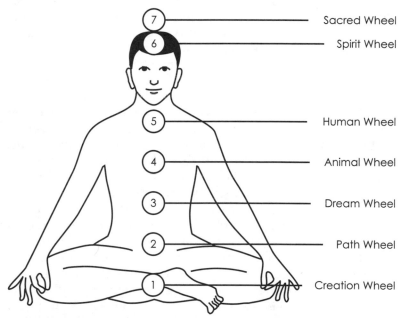

Figure 14. Chakras/Wheels in the Native American system.

With the "Dream Wheel," the world of plants, energy takes a further leap. Now organic change is possible. Minerals incessantly repeat the same patterns; plants are able to grow and develop in fascinatingly variable patterns. In our lives, the primal energy can now be used to develop any frame of reference we desire, any point of view. This is the world as a dream, the world which can be anything we choose it to be. Kundalini energy can get stuck at any stage as it advances upward. If it gets stuck at the Dream Wheel, it's because we can't accept change, because we have grown so accustomed to one particular view of life that we are frightened by the possibilities available for our lives. This is the stage where we experience the existential fear of the new that is such a common 20th-century disease. We feel this fear in the "pit of our stomach," where the Dream Wheel is located. When something in our life makes us feel queasy, or our stomach knots up, this chakra is involved.

In chapter 4 ("Synchronicity") I told how, when working with severely disturbed young adults in a halfway home, I would often feel their emotions flood through me. I believe it is this chakra that was awakened at such times (though some traditions believe this happens at the Path Wheel.) The patients were trapped in their emotional lives due to fear, and anger, and sadness. When we were in synchrony, a flow opened between us and, since I was less trapped by fear, the emotion poured out of me. Empathy begins at this chakra and becomes progressively more developed in the chakras to come.

Fourth is the "Animal Wheel," located in the middle of the chest. While plants can grow and change in seemingly never-ending varieties, animals bring emotion, individuality, communion, and much more into the picture. The Animal Wheel is concerned with heart-balance, the harmony of emotions so beautifully seen in animals. Here our energy is connected to the life around us. At best we can feel an animal among other animals, an integral part of all creation. At worst, we have no sense of ourselves as either higher or lower. But this is largely a centered place to which one can return in difficult times, or it can be used as a base of operations. This is the chakra energized by most of the humanistic psychologies today. This is where we learn love — self-love, love for another, for a group, a cause, a higher power. When this chakra is fully open, we find

ourselves expanding beyond our physical body, reaching outward to all around us. Not only can we experience the emotions of others, as we do with the Dream Wheel, but we can
reach out and envelop those around us within our love. The
actual experience is more that love is the reality that encompasses us and those around us.

The fifth chakra, the "Human Wheel," is located in your
throat. It represents a stage where, with emotions in balance,
we can be fully human. Here energy needs to find expression.
Often people are stuck at this stage because they have something to say and can't get it out. The quiet voice within often
finds expression at this chakra by allowing us to write, or
paint, or say out loud something that we need to know ourselves. Every creative person has learned to find what he or
she needs to know by expressing something inchoate inside.
I've found that many people have actual physical problems related to their throats when they are stuck at this wheel. It is
perhaps the most common area to be stuck in for those who
enter therapy.

The need for expression may come from outside ourselves
(after all, as we're finding in this book, the inside and the outside are interrelated in a complex self-referential loop). In my
description of the synchrony that formed between therapist and
patient in my work in the halfway home, I told how the normally painfully inarticulate "Jean" was able to tell me exactly
what I needed to know without even knowing my problem. As I
came to be more in control of the emotions of my patients flowing through me, I learned to simply let the unconscious talk
through me, much as it had through Jean. I'd tell parables or
fairy tales or relate seemingly innocuous events from my own
life or the lives of others, with no conscious knowledge of why
this was important for the patient. But, as long as I was in this
open state, what I said was invariably just what the patient
needed to hear. A famous family therapist, Carl Whitaker, used
to use similar techniques. One I've dubbed "fractured fairy
tales" (ala "Rockie and Bullwinkle"). He'd start to tell a familiar
fairy tale—"Little Red Riding Hood" or "Rapunzel"—but as he
continued, the story would take unexpected side-trails, totally
driven by his unconscious, until the final story was nothing like
the original fairy tale.

This ability to open ourselves up to the unconscious and allow the unconscious to speak through us is a powerful one, and it has several stages of mastery. At the lowest level, it takes place on an emotional level, as I explained in discussing the Dream Wheel. By the Animal Wheel, we are able to reach out with what is emerging from within. When we reach the Human Wheel, amorphous emotions can find concrete expression in words or art. In our time, we've seen this most graphically in "channeled" material, where some other entity appears to speak through a person. In a previous book,[11] I described a technique developed by C. G. Jung called "active imagination," in which we not only let something flow out from within us, we engage with it. As I point out there, the key that separates active imagination from channeling and possession is contained in the word "active." Not only do we open ourselves to the unconscious and let it speak through us, we then consciously engage with what comes out. This can be an actual dialogue—out loud, in our head, on paper—or it can be through other forms of expression, such as dance or painting. I will explain how to do "active imagination" in chapter 7.

Sixth is the "Spirit Wheel" located in the middle of your forehead (the so-called "Third Eye" so often mentioned in esoteric literature). This is the first chakra past the present human stage of development: the world of the archetypes. Problems at this stage often involve arriving at this stage with insufficient grounding below. When we start figuratively floating off the ground with our heads in the clouds, it's a sign that we've arrived at the Spirit Wheel without dealing sufficiently with the lower chakras.

Visualization opens this chakra wider and, since most esoteric traditions have extensive methods based on visualization, this chakra can often be opened prematurely, causing distress. When schizophrenics suffer an acute episode, or bi-polar sufferers go through a manic period, this chakra opens them up to more-than-human forces. Their fantasies, which people often think of as the cause of their mental problems, are actually desperate attempts by the psyche to provide some reasonable psychic "containers" for the archetypes that flow through them.

---

[11] Robin Robertson, *Your Shadow* (Virginia Beach: A.R.E. Press, 1997).

That's why it's so important to develop methods of grounding ourselves in the ordinary minutia of life, in physical exercise, in work involving detail. When there is too much head, we can start using the hands and the feet as a proper balance to too much head. The feet provide the "standpoint" with which we maintain our balance, both physically and as a complete being. Our hands are how we engage with the world, whether in work or creation.

Simply rediscovering how to play can be the best grounding of all. At a critical time in his life, Jung found, to his intense embarrassment, that he was forced to play building games, much as he had done as a child. But these were just what was required; they grounded him, got him past the point where he was overwhelmed by the archetypal forces emerging from within, and began to find ways to give concrete expression to these new ideas.

Finally, there is the "Sacred Wheel," located slightly above the head. It is easier to visualize this energy entering the body through the crown of the head.[12] This chakra represents the state of samadhi or satori. Interestingly, this is the "lowest" level of spiritual awakening in most traditions; more advanced states follow.

CHAKRAS AND BODY ARMOR

We run into the same situation in our work of breaking down the muscular armor. The individual muscular blocks do not follow the course of a muscle or a nerve; they are altogether independent of anatomical processes. . . . the muscular armor is arranged in segments. Biologically, this segmental arrangement is a much more primitive form of living functioning than is found in the highly developed animals. A conspicuous example of segmental functioning is that of ringed worms and the biological systems related to them.[13]

---

[12] This is the place where some traditions have drilled holes. This process, called *trepination*, is claimed to open the person to mystical insight.

[13] Wilhelm Reich, *Character Analysis* (New York: Touchstone/Simon & Schuster, 1972), pp. 368–369.

Austrian psychoanalyst Wilhelm Reich (1897–1957) was, along with Alfred Adler (1870–1937) and C. G. Jung (1875–1961), one of Sigmund Freud's most significant disciples. In order to understand Reich's major discovery, we have to briefly consider his mentor. Freud's work with patients led him to discover a dynamic unconscious mind that was largely a repository of repressed sexual desires. Since he was a 19th-century thinker, with the then cutting-edge mechanistic view of biology, he initially reduced the sex drive and sexual energy, libido, to a purely mechanistic process. As his ideas developed over his long working life, sexuality gradually evolved and came to mean practically anything that was creative, passionate, or driven by the body rather than the mind. But somehow he was still stuck with the belief that his broadened sexuality could be reduced to the mechanics of intercourse. There was a conflict here that Freud never fully resolved. If sexuality could be reduced to biology, it could not be all the things Freud wanted it to be. And if sexuality included art and spirituality and creativity and love and tenderness and much more, then it couldn't be the same as mere biological sexuality.

Reich was quite content to hold literally to Freud's biological beliefs, but made his own advance with the realization that biology wasn't a simple, mechanistic process, but an organic one. For Reich, body and mind had to be a unified system, and sexuality had to explain both sides of that system. He could never view sexuality as biological when that was convenient or metaphorically when the biological view wouldn't do. Nor could Reich view sexuality as a collection of mechanical parts — oral sexuality, anal sexuality, etc. There had to be one sexuality that could explain all these separate manifestations.

In the course of his own studies of patients, Reich discovered that they fell into basic character types. Because Reich's interest centered on the body as much, if not more, than the mind, he noticed that these character types have different "body armors," different ways that their bodies protected them from the world. Essentially he discovered the chakras from the outside in, by examining the body structure of people with various character types and psychological problems.

Since Reich wholly accepted the primacy of the sexual act in the etiology of mental and emotional problems, he dug deeply into the biological basis of the orgasm. In doing so, he came to discover the life energy which we have already seen as prana, ch'i, ki, mana, etc.; in his case, he called it *orgone energy*. His study of orgone energy was profound, but also one-sided, since he was so wed to the idea that foundation of this energy is the orgasm. The key fact for us to understand is that he found that the circulation of orgone energy and the achievement of a full orgasmic response by the body was usually prevented by blockages at seven different segments of the body. The different character types he identified had blockages at one or more of these segments, and the segments correspond in function and position to the chakras (with a slight modification we'll discuss in a moment). It appears that Reich was unaware of the chakras and the literature on chakras and life energy; he certainly didn't refer to them in his writing.

Reich felt that we live through our bodies, that everything we think, feel, or do is eventually reflected in our bodies. Our emotions are expressed in characteristic body positions and movements. Even thought has emotional overtones that the body mirrors. There is nothing we can do independently of our bodies, and nothing that our bodies don't record. Reich recognized both mind and body, but for him the body would always be supreme. Little wonder that, using Freud's basic premises, he ultimately came to different conclusions.

Emotions are expressed in our bodies—sadness may lead to tears, joy to smiles, fear leads to a knot in the pit of our stomachs, and so forth. But those are simple manifestations; actually our emotions are expressed in the body by an incredibly complex string of operations of which we have little awareness. I remember when I had to have my gall bladder removed. The pain that led me to check into the hospital was so intense that I was literally beating my head against the wall to try and forget the pain. I experienced the pain throughout my entire abdomen, even though the gall bladder is located about the middle of the right side of the body. When I asked the surgeon why I felt the pain in my stomach, he explained that the internal organs were a very primitive part of the body, a part that we shared with creatures that developed many millions of years ago. They had very little need for nerve endings as they were not yet conscious enough to experience the messages the nerves would send. So most of the nerve endings for the trunk and internal organs are concentrated in the abdomen.

The point is that we have very little awareness of much of our body. Most of our awareness is restricted to the body's outer surface. It is at that interface with the world that consciousness comes into existence. Of course, I'm talking of a primitive level of consciousness here. In this view, consciousness is a boundary condition. Boundaries are limits that separate the world into distinguishable pieces. We would do well to remember that the pieces are distinguishable as separate only because of the boundary between them; otherwise each merges into the other indistinguishably.

We are each composed of many such boundaries. Every body organ is a separation from the rest of the body and, hence, a possible site of consciousness, in the limited sense of the word that I'm using here. The body's outer surface is our major boundary, the boundary between self and environment. Hence consciousness exists at this boundary, the boundary we share with every animal down to the simplest amoeba, and, perhaps even with plants and rocks and subatomic particles. This diffuse "boundary condition" consciousness is an important part of our total consciousness and one we largely ignore.

In looking for the trail that emotional problems leave in the body, Reich found that the body stored these problems in segments, rather than continuously. Muscles and nerves are connected in endless chains that have no true beginning nor end. When we walk, we don't walk with our legs alone; our whole body walks. But Reich's body segments were separate and discrete, connected by function more than anatomy. As he said, "An armor segment comprises those organs and muscle groups which have a functional contact with one another and which are capable of accompanying each other in the emotional expressive movement."[14]

He discovered that the life energy flowed up and down the body (just as kundalini energy flows up and down the spine). Muscles and nerves, however, "armored" themselves horizontally, at right angles to this flow, to form body segments. The armor is like a ring around the body, fully protecting it from all sides, at specific points. Obviously, this is reminiscent of chakras, which are described in a variety of cultures as wheels of energy that form at right angles to the flow of kundalini energy.

---

[14] Wilhelm Reich, *Character Analysis*, p. 370.

Reich realized that this segmented structure is characteristic of much more simple creatures, such as ringed worms. In the higher vertebrates, only the segmental structure of the spine, its corresponding nerve endings, and the corresponding ganglia of the nervous system still have that structure. Paul McLean's triune brain starts where this structure, which he calls the "neural chassis," ends. So Reich discovered that our higher life, which begins with the rigid emotions of the reptile brain, continues with the softer emotions of the mammal brain, and culminates in the rationality of the human brain, is also stored in this much more primitive bodily structure! Hence the character armor segments, rather than seeming anomalous, are merely reflections of the fact that the body, brain, and mind developed out of more primitive ancestors.

Let's look at his segments for a minute. The first armor ring is the *ocular*, and controls the muscles of the eyeballs, the eyelids, the forehead, the lachrymal gland, etc. When the armor is on, a person wears a mask that prevents the expression of fear or sorrow. Reich loosened the armor by having patients open their eyes wide, as if in fright. A proof of the segmental nature of the armor was that muscle actions in this segment don't carry over into the next segment, the *oral*. If a person opens his or her eyelids wide, all the muscles down to the upper cheeks can move, but it doesn't effect the biting impulses which mark a blockage in the oral segment. Armoring the oral segment leads to a look of grim bulldog determination that cuts off crying, yelling, biting, sucking. Now, of course, the oral segment is connected with the ocular segment above and the neck segment below. Otherwise there would be no free flow of energy in a healthy individual. But the blockages are localized and lead to independent problems. See Table 1 (page 110) for an overview.

In summary, there are seven segments: "The ocular segment . . . includes the eyes, ears, and central brain structures. The next is the oral, centered on the mouth; a cervical segment, covering throat and neck; a thoracic segment in the region of the chest and arms; a diaphragmatic segment in the area of the solar plexus; an abdominal segment, and a pelvic segment, which includes the legs."[15]

---

[15] Ralph Metzner, *Know Your Type: Maps of Identity* (Garden City, NY: Anchor Books, 1979), p. 166.

Table 1. Summary of the Wheels and Chakras.

No.	Wheel	Chakra	Reich	Location	Description
1	Creation	Muladhara	Pelvic	Base of Spine	Primal Energy, Creation, Procreation, Sexuality
2	Path (Crystal)	Svadhisthana	Abdominal	Between genitals and naval	Choice, Power, Willpower Direction, Force
3	Dream (Plant)	Manipura	Diaphragm	Solar Plexus	Beliefs, Change
4	Animal	Anahata	Thoracic	Heart	Emotional Balance, Love
5	Human	Visuddha	Cervical	Throat	Expression, Speech, Communication, Individuality
			Oral	Mouth	Possible new Chakra or Wheel emerging?
6	Spirit	Ajna	Ocular	Brow ("Third Eye")	Vision, Fantasy, Aspiration, Higher Mental Processes
7	Sacred	Sahasrara		Above crown of head	Higher Unity, Collective, Unconscious

The lower five segments correspond exactly in location to the chakras. The ocular seems to correspond to the Spirit Wheel, but there is no muscle segment that corresponds to the Sacred Wheel and no chakra that matches the oral segment in location. It's sensible that there is no muscle equivalent for the Sacred Wheel since it is located in a space above the body. In many systems, it is seen as corresponding to the body's aura.

I would speculate that perhaps the oral segment is a further evolutionary development of a chakra intermediate between the Human Wheel and the Spirit Wheel. I know that in hand-scanning the chakras, I frequently experience energy around the mouth and nasal passages. I had previously regarded this as energy trapped between the chakras, but perhaps a new chakra is emerging. If I'm correct is this assumption, then Reich's segments perfectly correspond to the chakras, yet they were discovered by observing the musculature of the body.

MOVING DOWN THE CHAKRAS TO RESOLVE EMOTIONAL PROBLEMS

The concept of "armor stratification" opened many possibilities for clinical work.[16]

Love, work, and knowledge are the well-springs of our life. They should also govern it.[17]

One important discovery of Reich's that isn't known in chakra literature is that blockages in the segments (and hence in the chakras) have to be dealt with from the top down. It is useless to deal with a blockage at a lower level when one still exists at a higher segment. The implications are that the chakras develop from the bottom up, both historically and in an individual. Yet problems which are reflected in blockages of energy and muscle armor need to be dealt with from the top down. This may seem paradoxical, since chakras develop from the bottom — the most primitive — to the top — the most advanced. Unfortunately, in our development, we often leave developmental

---

[16] Wilhelm Reich, *The Function of the Orgasm* (New York: Touchstone/Simon & Schuster, 1973), p. 144.

[17] Wilhelm Reich, *The Function of the Orgasm*, quotation before Table of Contents.

stages unfinished, or sometimes even unvisited at all. In our own highly vocal, overly intellectual Western culture, for example, many of us substitute our head for our heart, our speech for our body's messages. This leaves unexpressed emotions, unacknowledged passions, stored inappropriately in the higher chakras. This means that we can't get to our heart, much less the feelings in our abdomen and below, without first removing the armor we've built up at the higher levels. This is why developmental problems need to be corrected from the top down, before one can begin once more to complete development from the bottom up.

Reichian therapists actually work on the body itself, loosening the body's armor, releasing hidden emotions in the process. In an unusual memoir of his time in Reichian analysis, actor Orson Bean describes this experience:

> Suddenly he began gouging at the sore, knotted muscle again and he didn't stop, and then I really hit the bed. I began pounding hard with both fists, lying there on my stomach, yelling and screaming and biting and having a tantrum. I tried to beat my way through the bed to get away from his hands. I sobbed uncontrollably. I cried harder than I ever had before. Then [the therapist] let me alone and I just lay there, sobbing deeply. Every time I took a breath, it felt like it went right down to the base of my spine and then I'd cry again—wracking, convulsive sobs. I cried for about five minutes and then I lay there with my face in the sheet for another five, involuntarily breathing those deep, deep breaths. Finally, I recovered and turned over on my back.[18]

In working with patients in a more traditional psychotherapy, I also found that I ended up working down the chakras in order to resolve emotional issues. Let me talk at some length about an actual case history in order to illustrate this. It is a commonplace in therapy to say that depression is a cover for repressed anger, but actually anger is often itself a cover for deeper issues. A patient once came to me suffering from an acute phase of depression. His life was in a shamble: his wife had left him, he'd lost

---

[18] Orson Bean, *Me and the Orgone* (New York: St. Martin's Press, 1971), pp. 45–46.

one job and was afraid he'd lose the new one. Life had no purpose: everything was covered with the gray, sticky feeling of emptiness that characterizes depression. Let's call him Bob. (In this account, the client's name and some particulars have been changed.)

At first, it was hard for Bob to even admit certain things, to say them out loud, even to himself, much less to his wife and others. Gradually, as he came to trust me and the process of therapy, he shared them with me. Like most such hidden issues, they weren't anything awful, just the sort of thing you and I conceal out of fear of humiliation. Once they were said out loud, the anger came. For a while, there was a lot of anger. Then it started to alternate with feelings of love and tenderness. By this time he was talking with his wife as well, sharing these unspoken issues, these sometimes harsh, sometimes caring emotions. She came back to him and his job situation improved. At this point, just as things were looking up for him, he started to have a lot of fear. He needed more comforting from me at this stage than he did at the start of therapy. I could already sense that there was a firm direction in this progression, but it was only later that I was able to see that it corresponded to the chakras.

I came to understand that Bob was moving down the chakras, resolving unfinished areas in his development. After the fear, he fell into an arrogant period where he was almost unbearable. Happily, I had enough experience of such "inflation" (to use a term from Jungian psychology) in my own behavior to know how to bring him back down to earth without destroying his newly-won self-esteem. Finally he started bringing up sexual issues, and we seemed to have reached bottom. But that wasn't bottom either. At that point, he felt the need for creative expression in art. Since, however, Bob wasn't really an artist, that slowly diminished and he simply found himself once more whole and satisfied with his life.

Bob illustrated just how patients get stuck on developmental issues at a chakra, normally one of the lower chakras. As they pass on in their development to another chakra, they have to make adjustments for the issues left unresolved at the previous, lower chakra. That in turn causes problems at the next level, and this process continues up the chakra system. And, of course, each stage of development presents unique problems unrelated to previous chakras. Every variety of situation is possible. One may have to move down the chakras one-at-a-time to get at a problem much lower, or the only problem might be just one level deeper than the presenting problem. Or perhaps a problem at one level doesn't have much effect on the next chakra, so that you skip a level as you move down the chakras in therapy. Or, as is most likely, there is no single problem, but multiple problems at multiple levels, to deal with. But the pattern of cure remains the same: start at the top and move down the chakras.

Let's look at Bob's situation in more depth. Depression is a problem of the sixth chakra, the Spirit Wheel, located at the site of the "third eye" in the middle of the brow. This chakra can be the site of a new vision, a new way of seeing reality. At its deepest level, it is the stage where one realizes experientially that there is nothing but psyche. We come to realize that all we can ever experience of the world is our own inner world, yet paradoxically that world extends beyond our own individual experience. This is the land of satori, samadhi, of the mystical unions that all meditators dream of, secretly or openly.

But entering that boundless land without the proper preparation can be a terrible experience. First one needs to have already developed a strong, healthy sense of self through numerous struggles with both inner and outer realities. Legends and myths tell us that, in addition, we also have to have some special gifts from the gods as well. The hero must eventually receive a gift from someone with more "magic" than he himself possesses. In Christian theology, this gift is "grace."

All the deeper disturbances of the psyche lie in this chakra. This is where schizophrenics find their strange worlds, their voices. This is where the manic personality finds the god-like entities that take over his or her personality and ride him or her like a cowboy rides his horse. Even paranoia peeks into this world, though much of its roots lie in lower chakras. And this is the dividing region where so-called "normal," "neurotic," and "psychotic" can all meet in depression. While Bob's depression was centered in this chakra, it wasn't the issue in itself; it was just the presenting problem.

The next chakra is the Human Wheel which centers on the uniquely human world of communication, of words (with apologies to ape, chimp and dolphin researchers if I'm wrong in saying this is unique to humans). This is the stage where words allow reality to be stored abstractly within our psyches. Though the debate will probably never end, it is at least arguable that thought and speech are contemporaneous developments, and perhaps even one and the same thing. Bob had to think the unthinkable, say the unsayable, to pass this point. He had to grasp that the problems he faced were his own, not merely visited upon him by outside forces. Once he understood that he was responsible for these problems, then he could cure them; he didn't have to simply lie down abjectly in the drooping posture of depression.

At the Animal Wheel, the anger that often underlies depression, appeared. Having said what he had been so afraid to say, Bob now could feel the emotions that he had always covered up before. And hot anger was the result. A great deal of anger had to come out before the anger yielded first to sadness, then to love and tenderness. The Animal Wheel is where we have moved beyond our purely inner world and now experience our feelings in the outer world as well; and the outer world is far too important to be blotted out by denial or fantasy.

Then we arrive at the Dream Wheel, where we learn that we have to change — to transform — in order to survive the variety of the experiences presented us by the world. That is a scary experience for all of us. It probably starts when we're babies and we're hungry and there is no lovely, tummy-filling milk. Fear grows and we cry, and then a bottle or a breast appears, and the world is right again. But sometimes we cry and no milk appears, no matter how hard we cry. That is when we learn fear, when we realize that the world is complex, filled with shadings, and somehow we have to adapt to all those shadings. I had to give Bob a lot of loving at this stage.

Now we are down to the last two chakras. At the Path Wheel, we are barely human. Here we are lost in childhood's dreams of omnipotence; here that omnipotent feeling has to accept limitation. This is the world where we learn to make choices. We can feel our power, but the world is limitless and choices must be made. The baby still thinks it controls the world, since all it has to do is cry to receive milk at this level. Here we divide things quickly into good and bad, right and wrong, with no grays in between. People suffering from bipolar disorder can never seem to advance past this chakra. Bob got "inflated," but since I was there to "ground" him in the realities of his situation, coupled with warm praise for all he had accomplished, he didn't stay inflated very long.

Finally, at the Creation Wheel, Bob arrived at the primal energy which he experienced as sexual desire. Remember how I experienced my gall bladder pain in my stomach? When we arrive at the raw, undifferentiated energy of the Creation Wheel, we don't have many experiences to categorize such energy, so most often it is felt as sexual desire. But for others, it might be experienced as a spiritual awakening, or an outburst of creativity. When Bob reached this stage and started having strong sexual desires, it didn't turn out to be the central issue, as Freud (or Reich) would have guessed. In actuality, the stage of sexual desire soon gave way to the need for artistic creativity, and that in turn soon gave way to a general satisfaction as he integrated this new energy into his life.

I hope that the above case history gives the reader an idea of how, at a stage of our life where we become stuck (often in depression), we need to move down the chakras, dealing with developmental issues in reverse order of how they originally occurred in our lives. Bob's case is a real one (though as I've presented it, it is general enough that it could fit almost anyone) and an especially clear illustration of moving down the chakras in order to resolve problems. Other people suffering from emotional issues may have more complex trips down the chakras, but they still fit this model. And it is important to stress that at any major point of transition in our life, we will normally have to go through such a restructuring of our total personality. These aren't just issues for others, but for all of us.

In the next chapter, we'll look at some tools and techniques we can use to develop psychic muscles, with a goal of ultimately being "trained practitioners" of the psyche.

C H A P T E R 6

MEDITATION

Life has a purpose, but a strange purpose. When you come to the end of the road and find perfect insight you will see that enlightenment is a joke. Life is a joke; you'll learn to understand that sometime — not now, but it will come.
— Zen Master to student[1]

I n our discussion of the brain, we have seen how there are several older layers that lie inside (literally, lie physically inside) the reasoning "human brain" of the neocortex. Dreams access those layers and can thus provide information not accessible through conscious reasoning. We've already discussed how dreams can thus serve as a gateway between inside and outside, and how each of us can set up rituals to remember, record, and work with our dreams. In this chapter we'll deal with meditation as another gateway.

I started meditating at a very tension-filled point in my life, a time when my philosophy of life was thoroughly materialist and reductionist. At that stage of my life, I had discarded any

[1] Janwillem van de Wetering, *The Empty Mirror: Experiences in a Japanese Zen Monastery* (Boston: Houghton Mifflin, 1974), p. 8.

"childish" mysticism that might have gotten in the way of a very outer-oriented life. In those days, my little ego definitely thought it was in charge.

Then I started having digestive problems—there is nothing like having to run to the bathroom before you've even finished a meal to get your attention. After denying that anything was going on, I took the usual next step to avoid personal responsibility. I turned to higher authority and visited a number of doctors who gave me every imaginable physical test. Uncomfortable tests like the upper and lower GI (gastrointestinal) series, where they put phosphorescent fluid in one or the other end, and watch it progress through your intestinal tract. I forget the term they used after all these tests to describe my condition, but in summary, it was "we've got no idea, it's probably tension." And that was probably as good a diagnosis as I could get with physical tests.

What I needed was meditation, but I couldn't get there directly. Meditation would have been far too mystical a concept for me in those days. Instead I found a book which presented a technique called *progressive muscle relaxation*.[2] Basically the idea was to either sit or lie on your back in a quiet, relaxed setting, then alternately tighten and relax your muscles, moving from the muscles in your feet slowly up the body, until you had visited every possible sight of tension. From the start, I found this to be helpful. Once I had learned how to use this technique, however, I knew it was just a baby step toward something else. Next I found a very well-written, scientifically oriented summary of information about meditation,[3] and progressive muscle relaxation gave way to a simple meditation of saying a mantra over and over. I tried a number of different mantras at first, then gradually starting using a traditional one almost exclusively ("gate, gate, paragate, para sam gate, bodhi swaha").

> The first important requirement in the task of learning to control the mind was to restrict its activity. . . . The whole secret of the Satipatthana method lies in the selection of a

---

[2] Herbert Benson, *The Relaxation Response* (New York: Morrow, 1975).
[3] Patricia Carrington, *Freedom in Meditation* (Garden City, NY: Anchor Books, 1978).
[4] E. H. Shattock, *An Experiment in Mindfulness* (New York: E. P. Dutton, 1960), p. 63.

natural field for these activities which, though restricted, offer the mind continuous occupation.[4]

Interestingly, while meditation considerably eased my digestive problems, they didn't go away. By that time, however, my interest had shifted away from the presenting problem to the experience of meditation. In fact, though my digestive difficulties gradually grew less and less pronounced, they never went away entirely. When I have periods of tension in my life, the problems pop up again to remind me of the tension. The difference is that the physical problems are no longer center stage. They have just become part of my total environment, a somewhat unpleasant given—like smog in LA—but also something that provides a measuring device that is both accurate and impossible to ignore.

Meanwhile, I was meditating regularly—after I had gotten past the baby steps of how to sit, etc. I meditated formally at least twice a day for a minimum of twenty minutes each time. However, I also meditated on an impromptu basis many other times during the day. I would say my mantra over and over to myself when I was standing in line at the grocery store, when I was walking down the street, or doing virtually any other task that didn't require conscious thinking. During my work day, whenever I got tired of too much mental exertion, I did a mini-meditation to refresh my mind. After practicing mantra meditation for a relatively short time, I realized that, at least for me, it was also just a step toward something else. I began to explore traditional Buddhist meditation: "sitting" and "breathing." Simple enough—just sit quietly in place and direct your attention to your breath. Once I started this process, I knew I had found the right mode for me, and practiced sitting and breathing for the next several years.

SITTING AND BREATHING

"To be able to concentrate well your spirit has to be in balance; when your spirit is in balance, your body has to be in balance as well. The double lotus is a position of pure balance, of real balance. When you sit in the full

---

[4] E. H. Shattock, *An Experiment in Mindfulness*, p. 63.

lotus, you just have to become quiet because nothing
else can happen. . . ."

"But isn't it possible to meditate on a chair?"

"You can meditate in any attitude," replied Peter, "but
one is best, and that's the one we'll teach you."[5]

Let's begin with the actual physical position of sitting. Sit on a
rug or a blanket, with a cushion underneath your buttocks. If
your body is up to the task, the traditional full lotus position is
by far the best position for sitting in meditation. Here, the right
foot is on the left thigh, the left on the right (or vice versa). Both
knees press against the floor. The body is thus totally symmetric, totally balanced.

Another reasonable position is to kneel with your legs spread
to the sides of the cushion and the bottom of your feet facing up-
wards. This position has much to recommend it, as it forces your
abdomen forward, which is necessary in all positions.

I never could sit in either of these positions comfortably. Instead I settled for having my right foot under my left thigh, my
left foot under my right thigh. Though also symmetric, this position isn't as stable as a full lotus, plus it tends to force the upright position of the body out-of-alignment unless you're
careful. You have to avoid sitting back so that the waist lowers
backward. The right size cushion under your seat can help here.
"In all these positions, the stable base for the body is a triangle
formed by the buttocks and the two knees."[6]

Once you're sitting in one or another of these positions,
push your abdomen forward and your buttocks backward.
When you sit in this position, the body's weight will be concentrated on a small area just below the navel. Your body should
form a straight line when viewed from the back, comparing
right and left sides, though not when viewed from the side,
since your abdomen will be thrust forward. In this position, the
body is most stable and the mind most likely to be quiet.[7]

---

[5] Janwillem van de Wetering, *The Empty Mirror*, pp. 12–13.

[6] Katsuki Sekida, *Zen Training: Methods and Philosophy* (New York: John
Winterhill, 1975), p. 39.

[7] There are many good books available to explain how one learns to "sit" and
"breathe." I would personally recommend Katsuki Sekida's *Zen Training* (especially pp. 38–52), but many other books have also been wonderful sources for
my own development.

A

The full-lotus meditation position.

B

The half-lotus.

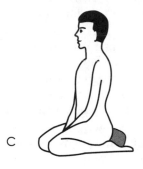

C

A posture in which the legs are directed backward and placed on either side of the pad.

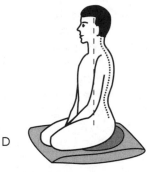

D

The spinal cord is not held in a straight line.

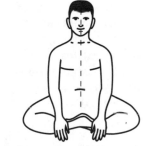

E

Relaxing and lowering your shoulders by placing hands on legs and exhaling deeply. An imaginary line can be drawn through the center of your forehead, nose, chin, throat, and navel.

F

The buttocks and knees form a triangle that becomes the base for the body. The weight is concentrated in the lower abdomen. The trunk is held vertical.

Figure 15. Various meditation positions. (Adapted from Katsuki Sekida, *Zen Training*, John Winterhill, 1975, New York.)

Now comes the breathing. At first it may be wise to use a mantra. For many, mantra meditation remains their preferred main method for a lifetime, though as I said, for me, it gave way to watching my breath. TM (transcendental meditation) practitioners are given a mantra that is supposedly designed just for them. In practice, however, this is usually simply one of sixteen TM mantras that are assigned to the meditator on the basis of age.[8] Though any word might be used, normally a two-syllable word is preferred. It has been noted that mantras often include *m* or *n* or *soft h* sounds "which seem to resonate through the head even when repeated silently."[9] Avoid a word that has strong associations for you. Thus a foreign word or even a made-up word may be preferred.

I've already mentioned the full phrase that I used most often: "gate, gate, paragate, para sam gate, bodhi swaha."[10] I found this especially good for times when I wasn't sitting formally, but instead standing or walking. The point of reciting a mantra is that it keeps your "monkey mind" (which wants to run around playing with all sorts of thoughts) busy, at the same time the recitation of the mantra falls into rhythm with your breathing. This is a powerful combination.

> The mind, so said the Sayadaw [another name for a Buddhist master], is without any inherent continuity; it is not always bearing thoughts, and it is not a form of unceasing energy. . . . Our thoughts are connected to one another by memory, inference, desire, attachments such as our likes and dislikes, cravings and fears, etc.; and it is these habits and attitudes that link each minute element of mind to the next, so that it seems to be an endless stream of thought pressing for attention.[11]

A variation on mantra meditation that bridges to breathing meditation is to count your breath. Simply count "one, two," then return to "one, two." "One" can be on the intake of breath,

---

[8] Patricia Carrington, *Freedom in Meditation*, pp. 77–78, 165–166.

[9] Marilyn Ferguson, *The Brain Revolution* (New York: Taplinger, 1973), p. 83.

[10] Obviously any one of a host of others might have been useful, many of which come from religious ritual. O*m Mani Padme Hum*, or *Hari Krisha* from the Hindu religion, or the Latin phrases, *Dominus Vobiscum* and *Agnus Dei* from the Roman Catholic mass. See Patricia Carrington, *Freedom in Meditation*, p. 83.

[11] E. H. Shattock, *An Experiment in Mindfulness*, pp. 89–90.

"two" on the out-take, or vice-versa. Soon though, you will probably find, as I did, that the sound of the count becomes intrusive. Your mind begins to demand more quiet, to simply follow your breath. Some observe their breath at the point where it enters their body, some at the point where it expands their abdomen, some follow the full path of the breath.

It's better to breathe through your nose than through your mouth unless you are a "mouth breather" who has no choice in the matter. When you first sit down to meditate, take several deep breaths through your mouth, then quiet down and begin breathing through your nose.

"Sitting" and "breathing" presented considerable challenges. Initially my body would protest at having to remain immobile for so long. When my body wasn't protesting, my mind was—no sooner would I direct my attention to my breathing than more interesting thoughts would come to mind. No sooner would I notice that my attention had wavered and try to force it back, than some physical problem would present itself. Even the experience of physical aches and pains is often a sign that you are advancing in your meditation. A master of the Satipatthana method of Buddhism explained it this way:

> While the mind was normally occupied with its myriad disjoined lines of thought that followed each other without break, the pricks and pains that continually occur in the body cannot reach the mind in their individual form; they are received, if they are strong enough, as a general feeling of discomfort; if they are not, they do not intrude on the conscious mind at all. But the continual checking of the mind by the practice of Satipatthana breaks this apparent continuity, and it is then possible for the conscious mind to receive and note each small physical disturbance as it occurs.[12]

In my early days of meditating, I was lucky to be able to sit properly and watch my breathing for a minute or two of the twenty minute sessions. I fought with myself, and no one won.

---

[12] E. H. Shattock, *An Experiment in Mindfulness*, pp. 52–53.

In time, the process grew easier—I learned not to struggle against the protests of my body, or the wandering of my mind. When my body ached or my attention wandered, I merely noted that fact, then directed my attention back once more to my breathing. This technique of merely turning your attention back to your breathing sounds ridiculous, but it works. It's a sort of judo in that you're not fighting your mind's tendency to go off on tangents; you allow it to happen, then return to what you're doing. If the thoughts that come up are impossible to avoid, turn your attention to them briefly, as if to honor that part of your mind, then again return to watching your breathing or reciting your mantra.

There are usually several different levels to this tendency of the mind to wander. In the early stages, your mind is likely to talk to itself continually. If you continue to direct your attention back to your mantra or your breathing, at some point, you will probably find that words give way to images. Often these are as sharp and vivid as those in dreams. Here is one meditator's description of this process:

> Suddenly, without my noticing a change, instead of thoughts in words, pictures flashed into my mind. When I eventually discovered what was happening and looked back to see when it had started, I remembered the first picture very clearly. . . . The unusual thing about these pictures, which I had never experienced before, was not only the vivid detail that I had observed in them, but that they appeared absolutely real. . . . Once I was aware of what was happening and watched out for being led astray in this way, they were detected and dealt with, just as the word thoughts, and they didn't trouble me for long.[13]

After quite a while, in my own case, I started to find that all these distractions largely went away and I could just sit and breathe. It wasn't long after that accomplishment when I found that my body would seem to vanish: I felt my consciousness diffuse throughout my body until it seemed to vanish. Or perhaps

---

[13] E. H. Shattock, *An Experiment in Mindfulness*, pp. 54–55.

an alternate description is even closer: my consciousness narrowed down until it wasn't there. Though the two descriptions—diffused consciousness or narrowed consciousness—may sound contradictory, in practice they weren't. There was still an awareness of self at some level, but that level seemed separate from me (if that isn't also a contradiction in terms). Zen Buddhism uses the word *samadhi* (enlightenment) for the higher stages of this experience. Let's call my experience a "little samadhi."

> "The empty mirror," he said. "If you could really understand that, there would be nothing left here for you to look for.[14]

Again this is very hard to describe. People experiencing various levels of advancement in meditation have recorded their experiences, but the experience is not readily communicable. One thing that did surprise me was the extent to which my little samadhi was physiological, rather than psychological. Perhaps I shouldn't have been surprised—since all the effort was at achieving a certain physiological state—but I was, and I suspect most meditators are when they finally achieve their goal. Once I had experienced my body disappearing, it was fairly easy to find my way back to that state again.

What I'd like to emphasize is that finding this place required a physical learning process on my part. There was nothing mystical about getting to a mystical state. I had to develop new skills—*psychic muscles*—in order to get there. Once there, I knew what the experience felt like and recognized the warning signs when the body was approaching the correct state. With that knowledge, it became relatively easy to return to that state whenever I liked. At the risk of being crude, it was similar to the control you have over muscles that you use to urinate. You couldn't possibly explain to someone else how you can choose to either urinate or refrain from urinating when it's not socially desirable. Whether you urinate or not is under the control of your mind, but it's accomplished by a definite physical process. Learning how to enter a state of *samadhi* (to use the Zen phrase,

---

[14] Janwillem van de Wetering, *The Empty Mirror*, p. 124.

and I'd again stress that I'm discussing a very small samadhi above) is a physical process, not a metaphysical process.[15]

CHAKRA MEDITATION

Feed your shit to Mother Earth. It makes the flowers grow.
— Irish/Cherokee medicine worker Harley Swiftdeer.

Sometimes it can be useful to impose structures around your meditation. For example, sometimes I begin a meditation by "rooting" myself in the earth. I simply imagine roots extending from the lower part of my spine down into the earth. I visualize the roots bifurcating into pairs of roots as they go deeper into the earth. I continue the process until the roots are so numerous and extended that I'm inextricably connected to the earth. I imagine the roots extending from my body connecting with the roots systems from the rest of humanity, from all life. Then I draw down all the "shit" in my system and feed it down into the earth through the roots. As I used to hear medicine worker Harley Swiftdeer say: "Feed your shit to Mother Earth. It makes the flowers grow." Once I can feel a clean flow of energy, I proceed with a normal meditation. This technique enables you to draw on the primal chakra energy of the Creation Wheel.

Another structure that increases energy for a meditation is to imagine wrapping a golden ribbon of light around your body, starting at your head. Curve the stream around until it slowly forms an egg, which fully encloses your body except for a small opening at the crown of your head. Once the egg is complete, draw energy down from the sky into the crown of your head, then breathe the energy through your body. When it seems appropriate, simply shift to a normal breathing meditation. Whereas in the previous technique you were drawing on the basic earth energy, here you are pulling in the energy of the Sacred Wheel. All that exists lies between these two extremes.

---

[15] For those interested, no one has done a better job describing the troubles and travails accompanying meditation than Janwillem van de Wetering in two books, *The Empty Mirror* (Boston: Houghton Miffin, 1974) and *A Glimpse of Nothingness* (London: Routledge & Kegan Paul, 1975).

You can combine the highest and lowest into a single structured meditation. After you plant your roots, as in the first meditation, imagine your body as the trunk of the tree with branches flowering upward from the crown of your head. You can even build the golden egg around the tree as a protection, with openings for both the roots and for light to enter and shine on the branches. (Or, alternately, allow the branches to extend through the upper opening in the egg and flow out to the heavens much as the root system flow below. Pull in energy from the sky, let it flow through your body, and out the root system. Then pull in energy from the ground through the roots and let it flow through your body and out to the sky.)

A more elaborate guided meditation is to breathe in and out through your chakras. This is a very powerful technique which can be used to quiet an overly active mind, to balance your emotions, or to generate energy. Simply sit in a meditative position that is comfortable for you. Either close your eyes or stare at a fixed point in front of you. Breathe in and out a few times with your mouth, then breathe through your nostrils and continue to breathe that way. At that point, switch your mental attitude to breathing symbolically, forgetting about the actual channel of the breath. Start at the "7-Sacred Wheel," breathing in and out there several times, then breathe in through this wheel, but breathe out through the next wheel, the "6-Spirit Wheel." (I've attached the numbers so you can more readily see the progression of the breathing during the exercise.) In and out, then in through the "6-Spirit Wheel" and out the "5-Human Wheel." Slowly work your way down the chakras to the "1-Creation Wheel," then slowly back up again. Depending on how it goes, this may be enough for your first time, as this can be a very powerful exercise. You may have to simply lie quietly after finishing it before you move back into normal activity.

Once you are comfortable with this chakra breathing, you may want to make the breathing pattern more intricate. Enter in through the "7-Sacred Wheel," out through the "1-Energy Wheel," in through the "1-Energy Wheel," out through the "6-Spirit Wheel," alternating above and below the "4-Animal Wheel" until you arrive at the "4-Animal Wheel," then move outward again alternating above and below. Once you master this so that you can move through this pattern without thought, then try moving in ever more complex patterns, sometimes concentrating on what wheel seems to need more energy, what needs less energy, where balancing needs to occur.

Though this exercise is complete in itself, you can add immeasurably to it by building up a set of correspondences held in memory for each chakra. There are many systems that provide corresponding colors, planets, tarot cards, and so forth for each chakra. Probably the most psychologically complete is the Kabbalistic Tree of Life, which can be grafted onto the chakra system and itself has complex correspondences. Just as a starting point for the reader, one common assignment of colors and planets to the chakras is shown in Table 2.

Though, of course, a great deal of thought and experience has gone into the assignment of these correspondences, you may still find discrepancies between, for example, the colors assigned by one system versus another. Ignore this and simply learn one or another of the systems with which you're comfortable. The importance is the fact that you go through the effort of building a set of correspondences for yourself, no matter which system you use. You need to learn a set of correspondences so thoroughly that, as you move through the chakras, they automatically come to mind without any conscious effort on your part. If you then allow the colors, as an example, to come to mind simultaneously with breathing through the chakras, your breathing will acquire a quality it would not otherwise have. The more correspondences that you have associated to the chakras, the more you prevent the

Table 2. Wheel and Chakra Associations.

WHEEL	HINDU CHAKRA	COLOR	PLANET
Creation	Muladhara	Orange-Red	Sun
Path	Svadhisthana	Rose	Mars
Dream	Manipurna	Green	Venus
Animal	Anahata	Yellow	Mercury
Human	Visuddha	Blue	Moon
Spirit	Ajna	Indigo	Saturn
Sacred	Sahasrara	Violet	Jupiter

mind from following its normal untamed routine of jumping from thought to thought. In effect, you defeat this action of the mind by imposing a complex structure upon it.

BRIDGING CONSCIOUS AND UNCONSCIOUS

When meditating, subjects tend to show a predominance of alpha waves. These waves are particularly prominent during meditation in the frontal and central regions of the brain. It is as though the motor were idling as the brain drifts along in a peaceful, rhythmic fashion. These trains of alpha waves are sometimes followed by bursts of theta waves. The Zen monks mentioned before showed an ability to remain for extended periods of time in "theta" without going to sleep at all.[16]

In our earlier discussion of dreams, we saw that dreams are highly active states of mind, often (though not always) characterized by theta waves. Zen meditation provides another example of a similar active state of the mind that takes place while one is seemingly totally inactive. During meditation, the brain waves of most meditators tend to be largely marked by alpha waves corresponding to a release of tension in the body; in more advanced meditators, alpha waves tend to give way to rhythmic theta waves. In fact, Tomio Hirai, who has studied the connection between the brain and meditation at great depth, found that "theta waves emitted during Zen meditation are more regular and their amplitudes are greater than theta waves seen in sleep."[17] Inexperienced Zen meditators take nearly half an hour to arrive at this state, much like it takes a dreamer a while before he or she drifts into a dream state. In contrast, experienced Zen meditators can drop almost immediately into a deep meditative state characterized by rhythmic theta waves. This might be seen as an indication that meditation is a more controlled, or perhaps merely more structured, version of the dream state.

---

[16] Patricia Carrington, *Freedom in Meditation*, pp. 46–47.
[17] Tomio Hirai, *Zen and Mind: Scientific Approach to Zen Practice* (Tokyo: Japan Publications, 1978), p. 106.

But perhaps even more interesting than the theta waves are the rhythmic quality. There is other research that seems to indicate that deep meditation can *synchronize* brain waves throughout all parts of the brain. For example, there was one set of experiments in which meditators had EEG leads connected to multiple areas of their brains. In addition, they each had a signal button so they could indicate which of five conditions they were experiencing: "1) body sensations; 2) involuntary movement; 3) visual imagery; 4) deep meditation; or 5) pure awareness." When they signaled that they were beginning either "deep meditation" or "pure awareness," their brain wave patterns shifted from alpha to beta (which as you'll recall, is more characteristic of our normal waking life). But here's the kicker: all the beta waves were *synchronized* in all the different parts of the brain! So something special seems to be going on when we get to deep meditative states. We'll see the same synchrony occurring when we discuss mind machines later in this chapter.[18]

I found another set of experiments that compared Zen meditators with Yogic meditators Yogis quite significant. When Yogis, in a deep meditative state, were suddenly exposed to some external stimuli, like the sound of a bell, their brain state didn't change at all. It was as if they were totally cut off from the outer world. In contrast, the brain wave patterns of Zen meditators, in an equally deep state, would show an immediate reaction to the outer stimuli, then an immediate return to the deep state. They were not cut off from the outer world, but let it flow through them to be instantly released. Dreaming appears to be more similar to Zen meditation than to the meditative state of Yogis. These seem to provide two limit-case metaphors. Yogis show how we can become independent of the world around us, while the Zen adepts demonstrate how we can remain aware of the outer world, while we go deeper into an inner world.[19] In Zen, "this is known as the way of *wu wei* (doing nothing) or, a step further, the way of *wei wu wei* (doing everything by doing nothing)."[20]

---

[18] These experiments were carried out by neurologist J. P. Banquet. See Patricia Carrington, *Freedom in Meditation*, p. 48.

[19] Above information from Tomio Hirai, *Zen and the Mind: Scientific Approach to Zen Practice,* pp. 95–135.

[20] Arthur Waley, *Three Ways of Thought in Ancient China* (Garden City, NY: Doubleday/Anchor Books, 1939), p. 74.

I have already dealt at some length with breathing and life energy in the previous chapter. I commented that breathing stands at the junction between those functions which we consciously control and those controlled by our autonomic nervous system. You don't have to think in order to breathe, yet you are able to take conscious control of your breathing if you like: you can hold your breath, or take quick short breaths in order to pump up your energy. In some esoteric traditions, you learn how to take conscious control of other normally unconscious processes: heartbeat, body temperature, etc. In the Zen tradition I was practicing, you bridge these two sides in a different way: you learn how to become conscious of your breath, yet you don't interfere in the process. Later — much later — I was to discover that this was the metaphor I had to use to deal with my entire inner life: *I had to become conscious without interfering in the process.* Or in the metaphor we have been using up to now in this book, I learned to construct conscious rituals for dealing with gateways that were beyond conscious control. This has been much more difficult than it was to achieve my little samadhi.

MIND MACHINES

> At times I had the feeling that I had suddenly been placed at the controls of some immensely powerful machine. It was as if my brain had been given a tune-up and was now working in new ways, presenting me with new thought, new ways of thinking, new capabilities.[21]

Physical aids to meditation are as ancient as the process of meditation itself. As we've already seen, meditation depends largely on repetition and rhythm: repeating a mantra over and over in rhythm with our breathing, or observing the actual rhythm of our breath. Dance, chant, and drumming are all so ancient that it is difficult to imagine any culture lacking any of them. Chimpanzees, gorillas, monkeys and other primates vocalize rhythmically, beat on their bodies and objects to make rhythms, move to those rhythms. Dance, chant, and drumming

---

[21] Michael Hutchison, *Megabrain* (New York: Ballantine, 1986), p. 16.

all induce altered states of consciousness which bring a group into synchrony. First the group's movement becomes synchronized, like the little girl we mentioned in chapter 3, who led her classmates in an unconscious dance around the playground. And outer synchrony leads to inner synchrony, opening gateways to our inner worlds.

Shamans, those earliest "trained practitioners of the psyche," use all three techniques, as well as specialized drugs and other tools, to induce meditative states in which they can journey into the inner world of their psyches to access hidden information. These techniques are as effective today as they ever were. Today we find teenagers and young adults up all night at a "rave" party where they are surrounded by hundreds if not thousands of other young people, contained within a constant envelope of extremely rhythmic music. This is music that evolved out of rock and rap, with an emphasis on the beat, then added a further rhythmic musical emphasis that is deliberately "technological," "mechanical." No wonder these events are so popular.

In a time as technologically oriented as our own, it would be surprising if we hadn't developed explicit technology to deal with our inner world, a world supposedly beyond technology. But we're not beyond technology, in part we're machines ourselves. Of course, we're living machines and we're much more than machines, but it doesn't pay to forget that we live in our bodies and our bodies are in part incredibly complex organic machines. The early generation of "mind machines" which have been developed to date, though primitive by comparison with our bodies, are still able to accomplish quite a lot.

Though the general population is still largely unaware of any of the mind machines, there is a substantial minority who have used one or another of a variety of them, in order to induce an altered state of consciousness comparable to that on psychedelic drugs in a legal way (at least so far it's legal). The most popular of these mind-machines are "light and sound" machines. You slip on a pair of "goggles" (usually wrap-around sun-glasses with tiny LED's inside), and put on earphones. Both plug into an electronic "magic box" which plays pre-defined programs of light and sound designed to induce an altered state of consciousness—to entrain your brain waves into any desired pattern of alpha, beta, theta, or delta waves. Let's look at the light and sound components separately, though they're normally used in combination.

The goggles usually have 2–4 very bright red LED's which flash in each eye. (There are also white, yellow, green and blue LED's, but red is far more common.) Even though your eyes are closed during use, the flashing lights are bright enough to be recorded on the retina and transmitted to the brain. In these days of special-purpose computer chips, the magic box is easily able to control the frequency and pattern of the flashing. Some of the boxes are small enough to fit into a shirt pocket, and even the largest ones are no longer than a hardbound book. Many such electronic boxes are now, in effect, general purpose light and sound computers which can accept new programs, either designed and sold by the manufacturer, downloaded off the web, or even developed by the user. These programs are supposedly specially designed to improve creativity, induce relaxation, assist in learning, improve meditation, and so forth. At this stage, these claims are more speculative than anything else, but one certainly gets very different experiences from different programs. The user is given wide latitude in choosing from pre-defined programs, then varying the length of the program, the intensity of the light (in general, the brighter the better), and the volume, tone, frequency, and pitch of the sound (more on sound later). These systems have become increasingly more sophisticated, and increasingly less expensive over the twenty years or so that models have been available to the public. Currently they range in price from about $100 to $500, though there are specialized machines costing much more. Like all electronic products, one can expect these machines to become increasingly more sophisticated and less expensive in the near future.

If all we saw were little red lights flashing, this wouldn't be very exciting, would it? Happily, our brains are very creative and those flashing lights are transformed into all sorts of fantastic things. Now people vary widely in what they see, with some actually seeing dreamlike fantasies induced by the lights, and a small number who see almost nothing at all. But most people see incredible geometric forms in constantly varying patterns using every color imaginable. Mandala forms are quite common, with every conceivable variation; e.g., colors shifting, rings of colors moving in or out or rotating. In general the flashing pattern of the lights is incorporated into the patterns you see, with shifts occurring in rhythm with the flashes. Strobing tiling patterns, like those of a beehive or perhaps an M. C. Escher drawing (more formally called tessellations) often fill your vision. Many of the programs are designed to create abrupt shifts from one pattern to another several times during the program. Most of the machines are now sophisticated enough to bring the machines to a gradual halt when they finish, so that you're not so jolted by the transition back into normal perception. And remember that the purpose is not a light show per se: the lights are flashing at frequencies that correspond to desired programs of alpha, beta, theta, and delta, so that you are relaxed, then energized in complex rituals (there's that word again), all intended to induce altered states of consciousness.

While the lights are able to flash directly at the rates of the various brain waves, our hearing isn't capable of experiencing frequencies at those slow rates as sound; they would simply translate into clicks. So a different technique is used—*binaural beats*—in which the left and right ears hear sound at two different frequencies. The *difference between the two frequencies* corresponds to a brainwave frequency. For example, one ear might receive a buzzing sound at 128 Hz (i.e., 128 hertz, or 128 beats per second), while the other receives a sound at 135 Hz (128 + 7). The mind hears the difference of 7 as a sort of sweeping between the two ears. This frequency corresponds to a theta wave, and the theory is that hearing binaural beats at such frequencies will entrain the brain so that all of its waves gradually become synchronized as theta waves. Some machines use *dual binaural beats*, which are simply two different pairs of frequencies, say 128 Hz and 135 Hz for one pair and 256 Hz and 263 Hz (256 + 7) for the other. It's hard to describe the effect, but both sounds are heard simultaneously with movement back and forth between them, which creates an eerie effect. There are even more sophisticated effects involving varying pitch, modulation between tones, and the smoothing of notes built into many of the programs.

I've used a number of these machines over the last fifteen years or so. I find them most useful as either an occasional alternative to meditation, or as a way to quickly reach a desired state—most normally alpha or theta—upon which the goggles and ear phones can be taken off and one can continue with normal meditation. They are also useful as training devices which enable people new to this process to experience the differences between alpha, beta, theta, and delta states. That way, when they are nearing theta, for example, in their meditation, they will recognize the sensation and can almost "dive" into a deeply rhythmic theta state. This is again hard to describe, but once you know the experience of a state, you can recognize when you're close and how to move deeper into it. This is similar to the early primitive biofeedback training to induce alpha waves, but the light and sound machines have the ability to induce virtually any brain wave state.

OTHER MIND TOOLS

If the doors of perception were cleansed everything would appear to man as it is, infinite. For man has closed himself up till he sees all through narrow chinks of his cavern.[22]

Another proven method for inducing altered states of consciousness is based on the Ganzfeld effect, a word originated by German scientists in the 1930s. In the 1940s and 1950s, an American psychologist, Donald Hebb, demonstrated that when we are totally deprived of sensory input, we experience an altered state of consciousness, in which we may see hallucinatory images, and experience intense emotions. More recently, scientists experimented with restricting only the field of vision. Psychologist Robert Ornstein found that a total absence of vision emerged in which the person did not even know "whether their eyes were open or not."[23]

---

[22] William Blake, "The Marriage of Heaven and Hell," in *Selected Poetry and Prose of William Blakes* Northrup Frye, ed., (New York: Modern Library, 1953), p. 129.
[23] Michael Hutchison, *Megabrain*, 1986), p. 252, for above information on Ganzfeld effect. *Megabrain* is the "Bible" on mind machines, and Hutchison their most vocal and articulate advocate.

In a laboratory, a Ganzfeld effect can be created fairly easily by cutting a ping-pong ball in half, taping each half over one eye, then shining a light source on the subject's eyes. With careful arrangement of the light, this produces an uniform, unchanging visual field. Outside of a laboratory, this is rather difficult to set up for yourself. There have been several sets of goggles on the market that draw on the Ganzfeld effect, more or less successfully. One used goggles with a built-in light source that attempted the same effect. Unfortunately, there always seemed to be light leakage which took away from the desired uniformity. One inexpensive pair I currently own uses goggles much like those used by skin-divers, with a translucent colored lens. You wear them facing a light source and try to avoid light leakage by staring off into the distance, several feet away from yourself. The unvarying field of vision tends to make your brain create visual perceptions to fill the void. Combined with the varied colored lenses, this can induce unusual meditative states. The effect can be enhanced by using the sound-only part of a light and sound machine to generate "white noise" as a constant auditory background. Though this is much less powerful than the light and sound machines, it is an interesting device to use occasionally.

Some biofeedback devices have become small enough to fit into headphones. They buzz loudly when you're in a beta state and become quiet when you go into alpha. More elaborate and correspondingly more expensive machines use headbands or electronic caps that record your EEG patterns and feed them into a standard personal computer, where intricate analysis is possible. Another feedback device combines a light and sound machine with a sensor that registers your breath under your nose. The light and sound vary depending on the frequency and pattern of your breathing. In general, I've found that none of the personal biofeedback devices are as powerful as the light and sound machines.

I won't go into many other devices that are based on more esoteric principles, often of doubtful worth—though it is wise to remember that some of these areas at the fringes of science may one day prove significant. All are exploring the edges where psyche and physical world meet.

MUSIC TAPES & CDS

Just as my finger on these keys
Make music, so the self-same sounds
On my spirit make a music, too.[24]

The earliest tools used to induce altered states were a combination of chanting, drumming, and dancing. All music changes your consciousness to some extent, but some music is more closely tied to its roots than others. Gregorian chant, which evolved as combination group prayer and a group meditative technique, is as powerful today as when it reached its peak in the seventh century. Its power lies in the fact that all the voices are singing the same notes at the same time, which again induces a meditative state. Other musical forms that particularly lend themselves to inducing meditative states are the drone-based vocalizations of middle-Eastern music, the ragas of India, Bulgarian and Tibetan throat-singing, and the chants of Native Americans, among others. Virtually every culture has developed music intended to calm the mind and open gateways between inner and outer.

There are many music tapes and CDs especially designed to bring about altered states of consciousness available today. They use a variety of principles, including the binaural beats mentioned earlier, complex systems of overtones, as well as complex rhythms in varying patterns. I've had positive experiences with many of these tapes and CDs, but I've found that in general the most powerful effects have come from music designed as music by musicians, not from those created to demonstrate scientific principles. Musicians simply make use of the underlying principles more complexly and more subtly. Scattered within traditional classical music are many such pieces. Of course, what works and doesn't work may vary by individual, but I'll mention several classical pieces that work for me and others including: Bach's "Goldberg Variations," "Music for Solo Cello," and "Musical Offering"; Beethoven's Late Quartets;

---

[24] Wallace Stevens, "Peter Quince at the Clavier," in *Modern American & Modern British Poetry*, Louis Untermeyer, ed. (New York: Harcourt, Brace & World, 1955), p. 100.

Ravel's "Bolero"; Satie's "Trois Gymnopedes"; Mussorgsky's "Pictures at an Exhibition"; Hindemith's "Mathis der Maler"; and to mention a lesser known composer who is a personal favorite: Messiaen's "Visions de l'Amen," "Quartet for the End of Time," and "Trois Petite Liturgies for the Divine Jesus." And, of course, Gregorian Chants and other *plain songs* such as the vocal works of the medieval abbess and mystic Hildegard of Bingen. There is an enormous variety of such music from many different European nations. The above selections are, of course, only a tiny sampling of the wealth of classical music that serves this purpose among others.

In our own time, there are many albums that can be used to bring about altered states of consciousness. Beginning with New Age music, then later with Ambient music and other offshoots, there are thousands of albums of what I teasingly call "zonk" music, since they leave you in a state of disequilibrium where it is easy to move deeper into the psyche. Some of my personal favorites include almost anything by Brian Eno, Harold Budd, or Jon Hassel, especially Eno's "Thursday Afternoon," "Music for Airports," and "Discreet Music"; Budd's "Music for 3 Pianos," "The Pavilion of Dreams," and "The White Arcades"; Hassel's "Facinoma"; and collaborations between the three in various combinations. An amazing vocal album that uses Middle Eastern drone techniques in modern settings is Sheila Chandra's "ABoneCroneDrone."

A great deal of jazz can serve this purpose. To mention just a few lesser known examples, Jan Garbarek's "Officium" is an inspired coming together of jazz saxophone and Gregorian chant. "Red Lanta," a collaboration with Art Lanta, also fits this territory very well. "Nigel Kennedy Plays Jazz" shows how an eclectic classical violinist can take jazz and drive it into the deepest resources of the mind.

Most minimalist music, especially Steve Reich, Terry Riley or Philip Glass is wonderful for yielding meditative states. As just one example, Glass' collaboration with Ravi Shankar on "Passages" is strange and beautiful. And much of John Cage's work is lovely and unknown to most listeners, especially "Music for Prepared Piano." A good sampling of his work, almost all meditative, is "In a Landscape." One of the most touching albums of recent years is "Sacred Spirits" which sets Native

American chant to thoughtful Western musical settings. Turning to another continent, Japanese flute music, such as Shakuhachi's "The Japanese Flute" is marvelously evocative. As with more traditionally classical music, there is so much that I can do no more than point to a few possibilities. And I guarantee that everything I've listed will "zonk" you.

FINAL WORDS ON INDUCING ALTERED STATES

In 1979, at a time when I had been meditating for about a year, I had an important dream that spoke to these matters. In the dream, I was in a cavern, participating in an initiation rite. As part of the ritual, a marijuana joint was passed successively from one acolyte to another. When it came to me and I tried to pass it on, it kept slipping from my fingers. Somehow I couldn't hold it long enough to pass it on to the next person in line. I became aware that I had to learn how to do it "by the numbers." When I did so, I was finally successful.

I think that dream was teaching me that it isn't enough to experience alternative states of consciousness. We have to develop control over that process—methodical, "by the numbers" control. This is hardly a new revelation. In every esoteric spiritual tradition, there is a stage of ecstatic union with the universe (or God, or one's higher self, or various other terms for the same experience). At this stage, everything is revealed in its own perfection. However, as soon as the acolyte steps out of the experience, the memory begins to fade. The world around looks gray and desolate in comparison. There is a temptation to keep returning to the ecstatic state in preference to the mundane world in which we all live. However, most esoteric traditions rightly regard this as merely an early stage of enlightenment—sort of an adolescence of spirituality. In order to advance further, one has to go back into the world and find a way to incorporate that same consciousness in the normal routine of life.

In the introduction, I mentioned the series of ten pictures of a man "In Search of his Missing Ox" that Buddhists used to picture the stages of enlightenment. The missing ox represents the man's true nature, which all of us lose and have to find again. At the start, the man is sitting at ease beneath a tree. He then notices that the ox is lost, and goes hunting for it. Along the way, he catches a glimpse of the ox, then loses sight of it again. Later he catches it, tames it, and leads it back. At the end, the ox has been recovered and the man is standing beneath a tree, talking with a fat, jovial master. Everything is the same, yet somehow everything has changed.[25]

Or perhaps even more succinctly, Zen Buddhist masters say that, before enlightenment, we are like animals who eat when we are hungry, sleep when we are tired. After enlightenment, once again we Eat when we are hungry, Sleep when we are tired. But what a difference between eating and Eating, sleeping and Sleeping—the difference between eating and sleeping unconsciously, and Eating and Sleeping with full consciousness! We have constructed rituals so that the gateways to the unconscious are always open.

My learning process has involved moving back and forth between such ancient wisdom (and sometimes ignorance) and modern knowledge (often arrogant foolishness). In both cases, a selection process has been necessary: I have had to distinguish the true core of knowledge from the outer trappings that every tradition acquires over the years. This process has been neither quick nor easy, and continues.

---

[25] See J. Marvin Spiegelman, "The Oxherding Pictures of Zen Buddhism: A Commentary," in J. Marvin Spiegelman and Mokusen Miyuki, *Buddhism and Jungian Psychology* (Phoenix, AZ: New Falcon Press, 1985), pp. 43–87 for a psychological analysis of these pictures.

SPEAKING FOR THE GODS

I am the silence that is incomprehensible
  and the idea whose remembrance is frequent.
I am the voice whose sound is manifold
  and the word whose appearance is multiple.
I am the utterance of my name.
                    —The Thunder: Perfect Mind[1]

T he *American Heritage Talking Dictionary* (1997) defines *divination* as "the art or act of foretelling future events or revealing knowledge by means of augury or an alleged supernatural agency"; alternately as "an inspired guess or presentiment."[2] If we dig a little deeper into the roots of *divine*, we find as a verb "to know by inspiration, intuition, or reflection," and as an adjective "of, relating to, emanating from, or being the expression of a deity." Hence "sacred."[3] So divination can be regarded prosaically as merely "an inspired guess or presentiment" or more profoundly as a way of "expression of a deity." But whether viewed as prosaic or profound, divination is a method to access information not otherwise available.

---

[1] Anonymous, "The Thunder, Perfect Mind," in James M. Robinson, ed., *The Nag Hammadi Library* (San Francisco: HarperSanFrancisco, 1988), p. 298.
[2] *American Heritage Talking Dictionary* (New York: Learning Company, 1997)
[3] *American Heritage Dictionary*, 2nd college ed. (Boston: Houghton Mifflin, 1991), p. 412.

Is there "something" inside us that is in some strange sense "not us," something that "knows?" Does "it" wish to convey messages? Jung felt that the unconscious had access to information that cut across boundaries of time and space; he referred to this as *absolute knowledge*. Marie-Louise von Franz argues that there is:

> . . . an *a priori* meaning in nature herself, existing prior to human consciousness, a *formal factor* in nature which cannot be explained causally but, on the contrary, is prior to any attempt at explanation on the part of human consciousness. This formal factor of meaning Jung called "absolute knowledge," absolute because independent of our conscious knowledge. It as if something somewhere were "known" in the form of images—but not by us.[4]

We have already discussed several gateways that tap into that absolute knowledge—dreams, meditation, synchronicity. Divination is one further such gateway, a powerful one. The forms of divination vary widely. In this chapter we will consider methods that quiet consciousness enough to allow the unconscious to speak through us. I've already told how, when I worked at a halfway home, I learned to achieve synchrony with my patients so that their emotions and later, symbolic images, flowed from them to me. And I told how, in a period of personal emotional strain, my patient Jean was able to access that absolute knowledge in order to tell me exactly what I needed to hear.

In our discussion of dreams, I told how Henry Reed replicated the ancient methods used in the temples of Asclepius to induce healing dreams. But the temples of Asclepius were Johnnie-come-latelies in comparison with the oracular shrine built at Delphi in honor of Apollo, which was already ancient by the time of the *Iliad*. It is mentioned in Minoan records dating back to 1500 B.C., though then the shrine honored the earth goddess Gaia. Its history stretched over the better part of two millennia, finally being destroyed in 390. It is a perfect example of our first divinatory technique—mediumistic oracles.

---

[4] Marie-Louise von Franz, *C. G. Jung: His Myth in Our Time* (New York: G. P. Putnam's Sons, 1975), p. 240.

DIVINATION THROUGH MEDIUMISTIC ORACLES

But the most celebrated of the Grecian oracles was that of Apollo at Delphi, a city built on the slopes of Parnassus in Phocis. It had been observed at a very early period that the goats feeding on Parnassus were thrown into convulsions when they approached a certain long deep cleft in the side of the mountain. This was owing to a peculiar vapor arising out of the cavern, and one of the goatherds was induced to try its effects upon himself. Inhaling the intoxicating air he was affected in the same manner as the cattle had been, and the inhabitants of the surrounding country, unable to explain the circumstance, imputed the convulsive ravings to which he gave utterance while under the power of the exhalations, to a divine inspiration. The fact was speedily circulated widely, and a temple was erected on the spot.[5]

The Greeks considered Earth itself to be a living being, and this site to be the omphalos, the navel, the center, of this being. The shrine at Delphi, a town on the slope of Mount Parnassus, was built around a cave or cleft in the ground from which gasses flowed. The Greek legend of the founding of the Oracle at Delphi is that Apollo killed the huge serpent Python that protected Gaia and forced her to leave the cave. He threw the body of Python into the cave, and the decomposing body formed the sacred fumes. Because of this story, the priestesses who served as mediums for Apollo were called Pythiæ. The fact that it was women who served Apollo here, rather than male priests as at every other shrine to Apollo, is, however, more likely due to the shrine's earlier history as a shrine to Gaia. As so often, as one religion gives way to another, the rites and practices of the original are incorporated into the new.

The priestesses were originally virgins who lived at the shrine and tended it, dedicating their lives to Apollo much as Catholic nuns dedicate their lives to Jesus. In the early history of

---

[5] Thomas Bullfinch, *Age of Fable or Beauties of Mythology* (New York: Heritage Press, 1942), Chapter XXXIV: Pythagoras – Egyptian Deities – Oracles.

the Oracle, the god spoke only once every seven years, but the need for the Oracle grew to the point that eventually the Pythia had to serve as the god's mouthpiece once a month. By this time, the priestesses, rather than being young maidens, were required to be over 50 years old. This change was probably because the maiden priestesses were all too often subject to molestation by the increasing crowds.

The Pythia who was to serve as Apollo's mouth went through an elaborate purification rite before each such ceremony. She fasted for three days, drinking only water from the sacred well at the site. On the day of the ceremony, she chewed bay leaves (also sacred to Apollo), then mounted a tripod that had been erected over the cleft in the rocks, from which came the fumes, supposedly of the dead serpent. The combination of fasting, drugs, and fumes induced an altered state of consciousness which allowed the priestess to "channel" (of which we'll say more later) Apollo. When the priestess spoke for the god, her voice became masculine and her answers had the powerful, enigmatic quality of all that comes from the unconscious.

THE DIFFICULT PATH TO WISDOM: OEDIPUS AND SOCRATES

One of the valuable services which a Greek looked for from this and other great religious establishments was, that it should resolve his doubts in cases of perplexity; that it should advise him whether to begin anew, or to persist in an old project; that it should foretell what would be his fate under given circumstances, and inform him, if suffering under distress, on what conditions the gods would grant him relief.[6]

The most famous story about the Delphic Oracle is that of Oedipus. His story begins one generation earlier, when Laius, the King of Thebes, consulted the Oracle soon after his marriage to Jocasta. When told that his son was destined to kill him, Laius tried to cheat destiny. He decided to send Jocasta away so that there would be no danger of a child. Before she could leave, she

---

[6] George Grote, "Pythian Games at Delphi: Part II" in *History of Greece* www.elibrary.com/s/edumark, from a book originally published in London by John Murray, 1854.

got Laius drunk and tempted him into her bed. The result of that mating was Oedipus. Once more determined to prevent the fate prophesied by the Oracle, Laius pierced his son's feet with a nail and left him on a mountaintop to die. A shepherd whose wife had recently had a stillborn baby rescued Oedipus and raised him as his own. In another version which perhaps found it unseemly that a prince should be raised as a simple shepherd, the shepherd took Oedipus to the King of Corinth, whose wife had given birth to the stillborn child. There he was raised by the king as his son.

Upon growing into manhood, the Oracle once more enters the story. Oedipus had been tormented during his childhood by other boys, who constantly teased him about his doubtful parentage. Finally he went to the Oracle and asks who are his parents? The Oracle tells him only that he is destined to kill his father and marry his mother. Oedipus, like his father Laius, tries to cheat his destiny by leaving home. On the road he encounters Laius and his servants. Thinking they are robbers—a common enough occurrence at the time—Oedipus kills all of them, thus unknowingly fulfilling the first part of the prophesy.

After further wandering, Oedipus comes to Thebes, which has been terrified by a monster called the Sphinx. It roams the roads into the city, stopping travelers and asking them a riddle. When they fail to correctly answer the riddle, the Sphinx devours them. The riddle asks, "What creature is it who in the morning has four feet, at noon two, and in the evening walks on three?" Upon reflection, Oedipus hits on the right answer: Man, who crawls when he's a baby, walks upright on two legs when he's in his prime, and leans on a cane when he's old and doddering. Unable to bear having its riddle answered, the Sphinx kills itself.

When Oedipus enters Thebes, the grateful city makes him king and gives him the widowed Queen Jocasta as his wife. They live in happiness for a number of years until the city is devastated by a plague. For a third time, the Oracle is consulted. This time the Oracle says that the plague will continue until Laius' murderer is discovered. Oedipus initiates an intense search for the killer. In the course of the investigation, he hears of the Oracle's original prediction that Laius would be killed by his son. At that, he realizes who he is and what he's done; he knows now that, despite his efforts to avoid killing his own father and sleeping with his mother, he has done just that.

Figure 16. The Sphinx is disgraced after Oedipus solves its riddle. From an ancient Greek cup. (Reprinted from Huber's *Treasury of Fantastic and Mythological Creatures.*)

His grief was profound; as Oedipus says in Sophocles' *Oedipus Rex*: "When I had passed the grave, how could these eyes have met my father's gaze, or my unhappy mother's—since on both I have done wrongs beyond all other wrong?"[7] In despair, Oedipus tears out his eyes, then leaves the city, wandering blindly, accompanied only by his daughter Antigone (who has her own story, which we'll leave for our readers to discover on their own). At length he arrives at Colonus, near Athens, where there is a shrine dedicated to the goddesses called the Eumenides. He is welcomed and allowed to make his home there; he lives in Colonus the remainder of his life, becoming a wise and respected man. He dies, finally at peace, after Apollo gives him a promise that the place of his death will remain sacred and will bring great benefit to the city of Athens, which has given shelter to the wanderer.

Freud centered his whole psychology on the myth of Oedipus, feeling that it was a symbolic representation of a story that is repeated over and over: all males grow to desire their mother

---

[7] Sophocles, *Oedipus Rex*, in S. Barnet, M. Berman, W. Burton, eds., *Eight Great Tragedies*, J. T. Sheppard, trans. (New York: Mentor, 1957), p. 89.

incestuously and hate their fathers for possessing her. But let's try and look at the story a little less literally than Freud did.

The myth of Oedipus in many ways fits the classic outline of the hero. Heroes usually have both a royal (or even divine) parent and a common parent. Jesus is considered the son of God, yet he grew up with the carpenter Joseph as his father. Heracles (Hercules in the Roman mythology) had both the god Zeus and the mortal Amphitryon as fathers. Oedipus is the son of King Laius, yet is found and raised by a simple shepherd.[8]

The birth of a hero is often accompanied by omens, and the life is threatened or the hero is abandoned soon after birth. Perhaps the most famous example in the Western world is the story of how the wise men foretold the birth of Jesus, "the King of the Jews," in Bethlehem, which led Herod to order the death of all newborn children in the region. But Jesus escapes. Hera sent two serpents to kill the baby Heracles. In Oedipus' myth, after the Delphic Oracle tells Laius that he is destined to be killed by his son, Laius tries to send his wife away to prevent her having a child, then when one is conceived and born, he leaves it on a mountain to die.

Heroes often have a physical flaw, which presages their eventual fall from greatness. Most famously, Achilles' heel. As a baby his mother had dipped him in the river Styx to make him invulnerable; the only part that did not go into the water was his heel. He grew to be the greatest hero in war until slain by an arrow in his heel shot by Paris. In Oedipus' case, his feet were nailed together by Laius. Though this damage was never explicitly related to his downfall, it nevertheless serves as a prediction that his downfall will occur.

Eventually, like all heroes, Oedipus has to go out into the world and face a series of trials through which he proves his worth. In his case, however, his brave fight with what he perceives as robbers ends in the death of his father, though Oedipus won't know this for many years. In quick succession he then himself becomes king and marries his mother.

Freud interprets the myth of Oedipus as the story of every young male's desire to destroy his father and possess his

---

[8] Because of that classic situation, that version is probably closer to the original than the variation where he was raised by the King of Corinth.

mother. Yet that interpretation simply takes part of the story out of context. The story started with the Oracle's prediction to King Laius. Since this is before Oedipus is even conceived, it is clearly predestined to happen: Laius must give way to Oedipus; i.e., the old must die in order for the new to come into existence. This is a formula that anyone who journeys into themselves discovers repeated over and over: no sooner do we gain a degree of consciousness than that level of understanding has to give way to something new.

Laius tries to avert his fate by a horrible crime—infanticide. Thus he is presented as someone who deserves his eventual fate. Oedipus' situation is quite different; he tries to avoid committing the two worst crimes imaginable in his day—patricide and incest. He's not trying to protect himself; he's trying to prevent evil to others. Yet he is equally unable to avoid his destiny. That is the nature of Greek tragedy; the will of the gods is beyond human ability to change.

Oedipus is able to answer the riddle of the Sphinx, who had destroyed all the men before him. His answer demonstrates that he has a deep understanding of the nature of a human being: first a weak animal who has to be cared for by others; later a strong individual who can take care of himself (or herself, for despite Freud's interpretation, Oedipus' story fits both men and women); then finally someone again reduced to weakness and dependence on others. Oedipus' own story shows each of those three parts: his brush with death as a baby who only survives due to the kindness of others; then the young man who is so strong that he can kill a king and his retainers, so wise that he can answer the hardest riddle of life, so virile he can take a queen to mate; then finally an old man blind and in despair, his wife dead, his kingdom gone, leaning on his daughter as he stumbles along the road. So in answering the riddle, at some instinctive level, Oedipus already knows his fate, since it is the fate of all of us.

But remember that the story doesn't end with Oedipus blinding himself in agony over his discovery of his patricide and incest. After wandering with Antigone, he settles in Colonus, where he grows in wisdom, finally dying as a figure respected by all. Another truth we all have to learn: along with life's triumphs come suffering and pain. It is only when we blind ourselves to the illusions of life—riches, power, fame—

that we are able to look within in order to grow in wisdom.

There is another famous story about the Delphic Oracle that teaches us what it is to be truly wise: the story of Socrates' trial and death recorded in the *Apology* by Plato.[9] Socrates was forced to defend himself against the charges of disbelieving in the gods and corrupting youth. In proof of these charges, his accusers pointed out that Socrates was constantly questioning authority figures, often doing so in front of the youth of the city, who delighted in observing this, as would youth in all ages. Socrates responds:

> But I shall be asked, Why do people delight in continually conversing with you? I have told you already, Athenians, the whole truth about this: they like to hear the cross-examination of the pretenders to wisdom; there is amusement in this. And this is a duty which the God has imposed upon me, as I am assured by oracles, visions, and in every sort of way in which the will of divine power was ever signified to anyone. This is true, O Athenians; or, if not true, would be soon refuted.[10]

Socrates explained that his actions had come about because a friend had once asked the Oracle at Delphi if there was any man wiser than Socrates. The oracle had answered that there was not. Socrates, knowing his own limitations, was astonished at the answer and went about questioning men he had heard to be wise in the hope of proving the Oracle to be wrong. Instead he found that none of those he met knew any more than he did. But at least he knew how little he knew, while they did not. He thus came to realize that the acknowledgment of ignorance was the beginning of wisdom. This was similar to the statement of Lao Tzu (of whose philosophy we will hear more in the next chapter) at roughly the same point in time, but far from Greece in China: "The titles of clever, wise, divine, holy are things that I have long ago cast aside as a snake sheds its skin."[11]

---

[9] Plato, "The Apology," in *Dialogues of Plato*, Benjamin Jowett, trans. (New York: Washington Square Press, 1950).

[10] Plato, "The Apology," in *Dialogues of Plato*, p. 28.

[11] Arthur Waley, *Three ways of Thought in Ancient China* (Garden City, NY: Doubleday/Anchor Books, 1939), p. 17.

Knowing that his accusers would never be satisfied by any argument he could make, Socrates answered their charges only because he thought that others might profit from hearing the truth. Having defended himself to his own satisfaction, he went peacefully to his death with the words "the hour of departure has arrived, and we go our ways—I to die and you to live. Which is better, God only knows."[12] Socrates had thus risen to a level of wisdom where life or death were less important than honoring truth.

MEDIUMS AND CHANNELS

The oracles are dumb;
No voice or hideous hum
Rings through the arched roof in words deceiving.
Apollo from his shrine
Can no more divine,
With hollow shriek the steep of Delphos leaving.
No nightly trance or breathed spell
Inspires the pale-eyed priest from the prophetic cell.[13]

Though poet John Milton thought that mediumistic divination died with the birth of Christ, the process of going into a trance or other altered state of consciousness, in order to obtain hidden knowledge, neither began nor ended with the Delphic Oracle. The earliest successful practitioners of this technique for accessing the deepest levels of the psyche were probably the shamans of hunting and gathering tribes. Shamans developed various techniques—including the use of hallucinogenic plants and mushrooms, auto-hypnosis, meditation and meditative aids such as rhythmic drumming and dancing—in order to induce an altered state of consciousness in which they journeyed into the spirit world to bring back information that could be used for healing or for divinatory purposes.[14]

---

[12] Plato, "The Apology," in *Dialogues of Plato*, p. 40.

[13] John Milton "On the Morning of Christ's Nativity," in *The Milton Reading Room,* Thomas H. Luxon, ed. (www.dartmouth. edu/~milton, April 2000).

[14] See Stanley Krippner and Patrick Welch, *Spiritual Dimensions of Healing: From Native Shamanism to Contemporary Health Care* (New York: Irvington Publishers, 1992).

These techniques went into decline as hunter-gatherer cultures gave way to agrarian cultures and what we think of as "civilization." But they survived to some degree within the roles of saints and priests, magicians, and mediums. Periodically, these methods would appear again within the general culture. There was, for example, a huge recurrence of these techniques in Europe and America late in the 19th century with the appearance of the religion of spiritualism, in which trance mediums contacted the spirits of the dead.

> In the seances at the fin de siècle, women became men and men became women. There was no limit to who one could be or to how many. Terrestrials and extraterrestrials swapped places and exchanged notes on their habitations. Plato and Socrates returned to offer courses in postmortem dialectics.[15]

In recent years, mediums have reappeared in the guise of *channels*. While channels might sometimes still contact dead spirits, more often they provide a voice for less easily defined personalities, such as beings from a different dimension. As with all those purporting to deal with such esoteric matters, some Victorian mediums were, and some current-day channels are, frauds. And some are simply naive true-believers whose information is of doubtful use. But also some few provide astonishing information that bears comparison with that provided by the Oracle at Delphi.

But no matter who or what they are contacting or channeling, the entities are regarded as "outside"; that is, as separate and distinct from the medium or channel. There is both naivete and wisdom in this separation of the channel from who or what is being channeled. It's naive in that it ignores the obvious psychological explanation that the entities are unconscious parts of the channel's own personality. But wise in that the separation helps prevent the channel from falling into the arrogant

---

[15] Sonu Shamdasani, "Introduction" in Théodore Flournoy, *From India to the Planet Mars: A Case of Multiple Personality with Imaginary Languages* (Princeton: Princeton University Press, 1994), p. xi.

assumption that they themselves are possessed of super-human abilities.

Jung felt that we should walk a tightrope in dealing with inner figures: realize that they are contained within our psyche, yet at the same time be prepared to treat them as gods separate and distinct from ourselves. The paradox here is that when we descend deeply enough inside our psyche, we encounter collective figures of enormous power who have nothing to do with our individual personality. I used to see this frequently when I worked with the severely disturbed patients at the halfway home I previously described. In some ways, all "crazy" people are alike in their craziness. (And, by the way, those I dealt with there much preferred words like "crazy" to traditional psychiatric diagnostic categories.) When they are not going through an acute episode, they are as individual and complex as anyone else. When they are experiencing an acute episode of schizophrenia or mania, suddenly the individuality drops away and anyone observing them experiences collective personalities largely interchangeable in their variety. This is reminiscent of the gods and goddesses of the Santeria religion (commonly called Voodoo), who have predefined characteristics that have nothing whatsoever to do with the personality of the person they happen to possess during a ceremony. A wonderfully apt image used in Santeria is to regard the god as the rider while the person is their horse.

When we encounter such personalities inside ourselves through dreams or other techniques (such as *active imagination*, which we will discuss later in this chapter), they are normally hidden aspects of our own personality. But at a certain "depth" in the psyche, this no longer holds true: the inside becomes the outside and we find personalities that are part of the collective, not of our individual personality. Let's look at some parallels in mathematics.

INSIDE AND OUTSIDE

Once upon a time, Chuang Chou (Chuang Tzu) dreamt that he was a butterfly, fluttering about—to all intents and purposes a butterfly. It did not know that it was Chuang Chou. Suddenly he awoke, and there he was, Chuang

Chou again. But he did not know whether he was Chuang Chou, dreaming he was a butterfly, or whether he was a butterfly dreaming he was Chuang Chou.[16]

Which is real—Chuang Chou dreaming he was a butterfly, or a butterfly dreaming that he was Chuang Chou? Is it possible to decide which is which? The branch of mathematics called topology asks a similar question. How do you decide which is inside and which is outside? It's easy enough with a simple figure like a circle or a square. But what if the figure gets more complex? For example, take a pencil and draw a continuous, non-intersecting, closed figure on a sheet of paper. Don't lift the pencil from the paper until you've finished the figure; that makes it continuous. Don't cross over any lines as you draw it; that makes it non-intersecting. Make sure that you end up where you began; that makes it closed. Figure 17 (page 154) is an example of such a continuous, non-intersecting closed figure.

A French mathematician named Camille Jordan proved that such a figure divides the surface into two areas—inside and outside. It's easy enough to see the part that's clearly outside any part of the line you've drawn. How about some arbitrary point surrounded by a number of lines; is it inside or outside? It's easy to find out; just count the number of lines you have to cross to arrive at an area which is clearly outside the figure. It doesn't matter what direction you take or how complicated a path. If you passed an odd number of lines, your point is inside the figure; if you passed an even number of lines, it's outside. (I've identified two points on the figure, one inside and one outside. Check the rule for yourself using these two points.)

Let's make the problem one level more complex. Imagine that the piece of paper stretches miles in each direction. Imagine that, beyond your vision in any direction, someone has drawn an enormous circle which encloses everything, including the figure which you've drawn. The area which you previously thought to be outside, is inside that bigger figure; therefore, the area you thought to be inside is suddenly revealed to be outside. Of course, it's possible that the big circle might itself be enclosed

---

[16] Ch'u Chai, *The Story of Chinese Philosophy* (New York: Washington Square Press, 1964), p. 100.

in a still bigger closed figure; that would reverse inside and out-side still again. So within our generalized situation, there is no way to determine which area is inside and which is outside.

However, and this is the significant part, *you can still divide points on the surface of the paper into two opposite camps.* It's up to you what terms you use for those two areas; inside and outside are fine as long as you remember that you're only talking about a limited frame of reference.

By analogy, the Chinese emperor may not be able to tell whether he is a man dreaming he is a butterfly, or a butterfly dreaming he is a man, but he can distinguish between the two states! Whether one is more "real" than the other is a meta-physical question that won't be resolved with mathematics, but the mathematics of topology does provide a map of how we can differentiate figure and ground, or by extension: conscious and unconscious.

Another basic polarity in topology is left and right-handed-ness. There is no way to make a left-handed monkey wrench into a right-handed monkey wrench—at least not in three dimen-sions! However, you can turn a left-handed glove into a right-handed glove by turning it inside-out. You can do that because

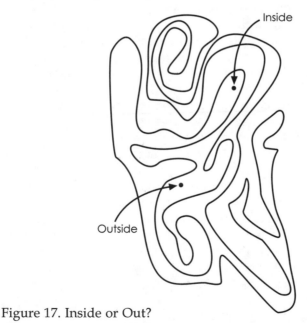

Figure 17. Inside or Out?

each side of a glove (inside or outside) is a two-dimensional shape. By turning it inside-out, we are using three dimensions to transform a two-dimensional figure.

Well, if we can imagine a fourth spatial dimension, we could take our left-handed monkey-wrench into that 4th dimension, turn it inside out just like we did the glove, and come out with a right-handed monkey-wrench. Nothing simpler, but we needed an extra dimension. As Alfred North Whitehead says, "I regret that it has been necessary for me in this lecture to administer such a large dose of four-dimensional geometry. I do not apologize, because I am really not responsible for the fact that nature in its most fundamental aspect is four-dimensional. Things are what they are."[17]

Take a strip of paper—say 1 inch wide and 6 feet long—bring the two ends together and glue them to make a circle. However, just before you glue the ends together, give one end a single twist. That single twist transforms a two-dimensional figure—a circle—into a one-dimensional figure: a Möbius strip (named after its discover, 19th-century German mathematician August Möbius)! Take a felt-tip pen and start coloring the outside. Keep sliding the strip along as you color it. Unless you've seen a Möbius strip before, you should be very surprised when you eventually arrive back at your starting point. There is no inside and outside, only a single surface that is both inside and outside. Note that an extra dimension was necessary; in this case, a two-dimensional figure had to be twisted in a third dimension in order to reduce it to a one-dimensional figure.

Magicians perform a trick called "The Afghan Bands," which is based on the principle of the Möbius Strip. Instead of paper bands, they use strips of cloth, which are easy to tear along their length. One strip is joined into a simple circle. A second is given the twist which transforms it into a Möbius strip before its ends are joined. Both look like simple circles of cloth. When the true circle is torn in half lengthwise, two circles of cloth result. However, when the Möbius strip is torn, you end up with one circle which has a diameter twice the size of the original circle.

---

[17] Alfred North Whitehead, *The Concept of Nature* (Cambridge: Cambridge University Press, 1983).

With four dimensions available, a three-dimensional solid can be converted into a two-dimensional figure called a Klein bottle. The outside of a Klein bottle is also the inside. If you fill a Klein bottle with water, the water would flow along the outside of the bottle onto the floor. Or you could just as easily dip the outside into a pail of water and fill up the inside. Unfortunately, we don't yet know how to go into a fourth spatial dimension in order to make a Klein bottle, so it remains a mental construct.

In dealing with the question of inside and outside, it is always wise to remember that something inside us may better be regarded as separate and distinct from us: within lie gods and monsters! And yet, we may trace a complex path that leads us into our depths, into regions that seem to have little or nothing to do with our particular lives, yet, as with a Möbius strip, we emerge again where we started. Remember again the Buddhist story of the ox-herder and the missing ox? Though the ox-herder ends as he began, he is totally transformed through the journey he undertakes. Because of this experience, common to all who go through the process of growth and change, we might rightly assume that there are many dimensions inside us beyond the three of space and one of time of the outer world.

ACTIVE IMAGINATION

The essential thing is to differentiate oneself from these unconscious contents by personifying them, and at the same time to bring them into relationship with consciousness. That is the technique for stripping them of their power. It is not too difficult to personify them, as they always possess a certain degree of autonomy, a separate identity of their own. Their autonomy is a most uncomfortable thing to reconcile oneself to, and yet the very fact that the unconscious presents itself in that way gives us the best means of handling it.[18]

As an adjunct to dreamwork, Jung developed a technique he called *active imagination* that allows anyone to consult an oracle

---

[18] C. G. Jung, *Memories, Dreams, Reflections*, revised edition (New York: Pantheon Books, 1973), p. 187.

within themselves. Active imagination is a process of consciously dialoguing with our unconscious "for the production of those contents of the unconscious which lie, as it were, immediately below the threshold of consciousness and, when intensified, are the most likely to erupt spontaneously into the conscious mind."[19] Someone who has learned active imagination is thus able to take some degree of control over his or her own growth process.

When the oracle was consulted at Delphi, the priestess — the Pythia — became totally receptive to whatever flowed through her. Her role was simply to be a mouthpiece for Apollo. In contrast, in active imagination, we have to alternate between total receptivity — to allow the unconscious to speak through us — and a conscious engagement with the unconscious. It is the alternation between the two which is unique to Jung's method, and which makes it so useful a tool.

As with all oracular systems, start the process with reverence. Only use active imagination when something significant needs to be discovered, and only when you have already exhausted your conscious resources. Find a time and a place where you can be alone, then take a few moments to calm your mind. Once you feel relaxed, use one of two basic ways to access the unconscious — visual or oral.

For the visual method, close your eyes, then begin with some visual starting point, perhaps a scene in a recent dream that has significance for the issue at hand. Get this starting point as clearly in your mind as you can make it, then let it unfold as it likes. If you are strongly visual, you may find that the resulting fantasy is virtually as vivid as a dream. The difference is that, because you are awake, you can consciously engage with the figures in the dream. As with any other encounter with the inner world, you need to walk a narrow path so that you remain receptive to whatever the unconscious produces, yet are able to react with conscious intent.

---

[19] C. G. Jung (1916/1958), "The Transcendent Function," in *The Structure and Dynamics of the Psyche*, Collected Works, vol. 8: Bollingen Series XX, 2nd edition (Princeton: Princeton University Press, 1969), prefatory note preceding ¶ 131.

In the oral technique, you engage in a dialogue with a person or object who you feel might help you with the issue at hand. You can actually talk out loud, hold the dialogue in your head, or simply write both sides of the dialogue. I normally sit at the computer, slow my breathing and stop my monkey mind as much as I can. I then type a question to, for example, an enigmatic dream figure from a recent dream. Having begun the dialogue, I remain receptive to whatever emerges from within and simply type what comes out. After allowing the inner voice to speak as long as it likes, I shift back to my own personality and react to what has been said. The dialogue continues in that manner.

You may find that you actually hear the words coming from the unconscious, or they may simply come out in the writing, without any intermediate process of hearing. When I use either the visual or oral techniques, I normally "see" only vaguely, or "hear" not at all, but somehow fill in what is missing through "feelings" in my body. Jung experienced the same thing: "Sometimes it was as if I were hearing it with my ears, sometimes feeling it with my mouth, as if my tongue were formulating words; now and then I heard myself whispering aloud. Below the threshold of consciousness everything was seething with life."[20]

Jung only came to this method after a great deal of struggle. At first, you may feel foolish trying either of these methods, but if you do, you will probably surprise yourself with how easy it is to allow this process to occur. When using the visual technique, you will find that the initial dream scene used as a starting point evolves in directions you could never have predicted. Similarly, when using the oral technique, you will find that the voice and character of the dream figure is sharply distinct from your own, and that you won't be able to predict the direction the dialogue will take. This lack of control can make you as uncomfortable as it did Jung: "One of the greatest difficulties for me lay in dealing with my negative feelings. I was voluntarily submitting myself to emotions of which I could not really approve, and I was writing down fantasies which often struck me as nonsense, and toward which I had strong resistances."[21]

---

[20] C. G. Jung, *Memories, Dreams, Reflections*, p. 178.
[21] C. G. Jung, *Memories, Dreams, Reflections*, p. 178.

I've already said that one has to walk a tightrope in using active imagination. One danger is that we don't open ourselves sufficiently to the unconscious, but instead edit what comes out before it has had a chance to really emerge. Or we may start interpreting what this all means instead of simply remaining open to what is emerging. We need to just let what wants to come out, come out. Jung argued strongly that the experience came first and the interpretation only afterward, if at all.

> We can try our hand at interpreting these fantasies if we like....But it is of vital importance that he should experience them to the full and, in so far as intellectual understanding them belongs to the totality of the experience, also understand them. Yet I would not give priority to understanding. . . . For the important thing is not to interpret and understand the fantasies, but primarily to experience them.[22]

The opposite danger is perhaps more prevalent. We can become so enamored with the fantasies or dialogues that emerge from within that we don't really take them seriously as something with which we have to struggle. This can happen equally with dreamwork. We can simply become fascinated at an aesthetic level and never realize that we are being presented with a challenge to our values. Again Jung was aware of this danger.

> A further danger, in itself harmless, is that, though authentic contents may be produced, the patient evinces an exclusively aesthetic interest in them and consequently remains stuck in an all-enveloping phantasmagoria, so that once more nothing is gained. The meaning and value of these fantasies are revealed only through their integration into the personality as a whole — that is to say, at the moment when one is confronted not only with what they mean but also with their moral demands.[23]

---

[22] C. G. Jung (1916/1935), "The Relations Between the Ego and the Unconscious," *Two Essays on Analytical Psychology*, Collected Works, vol. 7:, Bollingen Series XX, 2nd edition (Princeton: Princeton University Press, 1953/1966), ¶ 342.

[23] C. G. Jung (1916/1958), *The Structure and Dynamics of the Psyche*, prefatory note preceding ¶ 131.

Finally, I would be remiss if I didn't mention that active imagination is exactly the wrong method to use if one is already unstable and having a hard time separating reality from fantasy. Most active imagination is with personified aspects of your own personality. When you are encountering such figures, it is much like encountering others in the normal course of life. However, as I've already indicated, as you access deeper parts of the inner world, the people and situations become collective and cease to have anything to do with your individual personality. It's not surprising that the ancients regarded these messages from within as coming from a god without. The unconscious often speaks like a god, which may make you feel uncomfortable or doubt that you can trust what is being said. As a modern man, Jung initially found this irritating: "Archetypes speak the language of high rhetoric, even of bombast. It is a style I find embarrassing; it grates on my nerves, as when someone draws his nails down a plaster wall, or scrapes his knife against a plate."[24] But it is exactly that quality that indicates that you are indeed tapping truly unconscious material.

For someone who is less stable, instead of merely becoming uncomfortable, they may actually be *possessed* by the more-than-human energy that emerges. Jung says that sometimes "the subliminal contents already possess such a high energy that, when afforded an outlet by active imagination, they may overpower the conscious mind and take possession of the personality."[25] To the extent, however, that "active imagination" is truly active — that is, that we engage consciously with the material, possession is highly unlikely. More likely is that we fail to remember that what is emerging is not us, but some collective power. We get *inflated*, puffed-up with the godlike energy that we feel. Or alternately, we may get *depressed*; in that case, accessing the unconscious demands so much energy that there is little left for consciousness. Cycles of inflation and depression are a normal part of life for anyone who digs into his or her inner world.

---

[24] C. G. Jung, *Memories, Dreams, Reflections,* p. 178.
[25] C. G. Jung, *The Structure and Dynamics of the Psyche,* prefatory note between ¶130–131.

But over time, we learn both to recognize when we are inflated or depressed, and to dampen the extent of either. One excellent way to ground this process is simply to take the time to write the active imagination down in some sort of a journal so that you can refer back to it, just as you would a dream. I keep a combined journal of dreams and active imagination, with short biographical journal entries as well for each date. Active imagination is an incredibly powerful method for gaining access to information unavailable to consciousness. Those who try it will discover that each of us possesses an Oracle within who can be questioned in times of transition or difficulty. The next chapter will discuss another method of consulting the Oracle: the I Ching.

THE I CHING AND OTHER ORACLES

Of the ancient works, possible the true cradle of Chinese philosophy is the Pa Kua or "Eight Trigrams," consisting of various combinations of straight lines arranged in a circle. . . . The Eight Trigrams symbolized the eight fundamental elements or factors of the universe (Heaven, Earth, Thunder, Water, Mountain, Wind, Fire, Marshes) and the different abstract attributes that would be suggested and associated with them. Later the Eight Trigrams were combined until there were Sixty-four Hexagrams — each supposed to symbolize one or more phenomena of the universe, either natural or human. Together the hexagrams were supposed to represent symbolically all that had happened in the universe.

—Chu Chai[1]

F rom at least the time of the scientific revolution in the 17th century, we have become accustomed to the idea that every effect has a cause, that everything that happens can be reduced to a chain of events that unfold over time, each event leading ineluctably to another. But while this assumption of linear causality has been remarkably productive for science, it is a vast over-simplification. In actuality, everything in the world is connected to everything else in complex ways that don't fit readily into linear chains of cause-and-effect. As psychiatrist and mathematician William Sulis (who we mentioned in our discussion of saliency) says, "Many things in this universe of ours are under-determined. The information at hand

---

[1] Ch'u Chai, *The Story of Chinese Philosophy* (New York: Washington Square Press, 1964), pp. xx–xxi.

is generally insufficient to follow accurately all of the causal links involved in creating it. Instead, we extract from each experience that which is salient for us, and move on. One man's salience is another man's noise."[2]

SIX DEGREES OF KEVIN BACON

In the heaven of Indra there is said to be a network of pearls so arranged that if you look at one you see all the others reflected in it. In the same way, each object in the world is not merely itself but involves every other object, and in fact *is* every other object.[3]

Even when the chains are linear, they can be so strange and unexpected that reducing them to this particular way of describing reality becomes almost ludicrous. For example, John Guare's play (later a movie) "Six Degrees of Separation" was based on the premise that any two people in the world could be connected through a chain of, at most, six connections (for example, if I've never met you, but we have a friend in common, there are two degrees of separation). Still more recently, there has been a humorous game drawing on the same premise called "Six Degrees of Kevin Bacon," which claimed that any actor or actress, living or dead, could be linked to actor Kevin Bacon through at most six such connections through movies or plays. For example, Rudolph Valentino has a "Bacon Number" of 3, since Rudolph Valentino was in "The Eagle" (1925) with Russell Simpson, who was in "Broken Lance" (1954) with Robert Wagner, who appeared with Kevin Bacon in "Wild Things" (1998). The department of computer science at the University of Virginia has actually put up a web site[4] where you can enter the name of any actor or actress—355,230 actors and actresses are contained in the database—and the "Bacon Number" will be calculated. This mammoth task revealed that the premise of at

---

[2] William Sulis, private communication.

[3] Sarah Voss, *What Number is God: Metaphors, Metaphysics, Metamathematics, and the Nature of Things* (New York: SUNY Press, 1995), p. 108.

[4] http://www.cs.virginia.edu/cgi.bin/oracle/center-cgi?who=Kevin+Bacon

most six degrees of separation isn't totally true: 65 actors required 7 degrees of separation from Kevin Bacon, and 2 actually had a Bacon number of 8.

There is a profound realization hidden within this silliness: in the world we actually live in, as opposed to the world as simplified for the convenience of science, everything is connected to everything else in complex networks. Remember the neural nets in the chapter on the brain? The world itself is structured in much the same way. The world is more related than separated, and the relationships are not simply causal! Almost anything can be connected with almost anything else in strange, unpredictable ways. In chapter 3, we discussed synchronicity, which deals with the subset of acausal connections where the link is through meaning, or as we generalized it, through saliency. Since our earliest days, men and women have tried to find ways to capture the meaning hidden within events. Because we view the world as interconnected, we look for patterns in events we dismiss as random.

Looking for meaning within seeming chaos is an extension of the trance mediumship we discussed in the previous chapter. Rather than quieting our rational minds with autohypnosis, meditation, or hallucinatory drugs, we overwhelm it with randomness (or at least so much complexity that it appears random). The brain continually works to discover meaning in the world around us. In our discussion of the brain, we saw how we have not one brain but several brains, which store "programs" that have been useful throughout the history of animal development within their structure. Baby goslings are born ready to look to the first living creature they see as "mother." Magpies are born already knowing that cats and foxes are enemies who should be avoided. But those stored programs have to be adaptable to changing circumstances; new programs have to be able to be constructed out of old parts. As Gerald Edelman argued: "An individual animal endowed with a richly structured brain must also adapt without instruction to a complex environment to form perceptual categories or an internal taxonomy governing its further responses to the world.[5] We saw how neural nets approximate the way this process operates in our brains.

---

[5] Gerald M. Edelman, *Neural Darwinism* (New York: Basic Books), pp. 8–9.

In other words, we are born into a world that is so complex that it approximates chaos to a newborn; the brain brings order out of chaos by adapting predefined structures within itself. Rather than just seeing something black which moves, a jackdaw sees danger and springs into action. Without these abilities built into the neurological structure of all living creatures, they would never live, love, and have children to perpetuate the species.

And remember that since every living creature has a neurological structure that allows it to fit into the world, over time the relationships within and the relationships without become so intertwined that it is difficult to separate the world into separate parts. Everything and everyone are linked in lovely arabesques of relationship. One expression of this can be traced back at least as far as Lao Tzu. It has been restated variously by Plato, Xenophanes, French theologian Alain de Lille, Dante, astronomer Giordano Bruno, philosopher/scientist Francis Bacon, even American transcendentalist Ralph Waldo Emerson. Perhaps the clearest expression was by mathematician and philosopher Blaise Pascal, who is quoted in the introduction to this book. Pascal said that "It [where it might be nature, the universe, God] is an infinite sphere, the center of which is everywhere, the circumference nowhere."[6]

Linked within this exquisite order, oracular systems which impose order on randomness seem not ridiculous, as reductionist science would have it, but profound attempts to recognize that order. If an issue is important enough, the unconscious becomes engaged. The unconscious appears to be a perfect example of "an infinite sphere, the center of which is everywhere." It seemingly has no limits in time and space in arriving at needed information. The only difficulty is finding a systematic way to present that information to consciousness. Dreams are one such system that has evolved within the very structure of our brain over the last quarter of a billion years![7] Meditation is

---

[6] Above history from Jorge Luis Borges, "Pascal's Sphere," in *Other Inquisitions: 1937–1952* (Austin: University of Texas Press, 1965), pp. 6–9.

[7] Whenever dreams are dismissed as meaningless, I have to laugh at the thought that something has evolved over such a long period of time for no purpose.

another system which, while not as ancient as dreams; is at least as ancient as human beings. One purpose of meditation is to provide conscious access to information normally only available in dreams. One extension of meditation—Jung's active imagination—provides an example of a system explicitly designed to provide dream-like information in waking life. But there are many others.

ORDER WITHIN CHAOS

Looking at a chaotic pattern is like putting one's mind to sleep for a minute and getting information about what one is fantasying or dreaming about in the unconscious. Through the absolute knowledge in the unconscious one gets information about one's inner and outer situation.[8]

One of the earliest methods discovered depended on the brain's ability to discover order within chaos. This is the principle used by someone staring into a crystal ball or one of its many variations, such as a pool of water, or a bowl of ink. As we observe the random patterns of light within a crystal ball, a meditative state is gradually induced which shuts down conscious thought. As the brain struggles to find some order, the unconscious projects a pattern that has already formed inside, outside onto the near randomness of the crystal ball. The crystal ball allows us to dream, while awake.

One advance was the idea of developing easily replicable methods of generating randomness, such as observing the patterns formed by tea leaves in a cup after the tea has been poured out. It takes a good deal of training to even let patterns emerge while staring into a crystal ball. But anyone can observe the patterns left by tea leaves in a cup. The skill then becomes the interpretation of those patterns. If there is a structure within the world which is modeled within the structure of the brain, then the same patterns of tea leaves should bring up the same inner structures, at least for two equally

---

[8] Marie-Louise von Franz, *On Divination and Synchronicity: The Psychology of Meaningful Coincidence* (Toronto: Inner City Books, 1980), p. 41.

skilled "trained practitioners of the psyche." And, in fact, that proved true. Exposed to the same patterns, shamans would come up with similar interpretations.

Then, of course, it was only reasonable to record, normally orally in the earlier traditions, the meanings various *seers* imposed on the patterns. Over time, those interpretations which proved most effective became codified into systems of patterns that could be learned by those who desired to be trained in these divinatory techniques.

Some of the best-known systems are numerology, cheiromancy (palm-reading), astrology, and divination with playing cards, especially with the tarot deck. But there have been many others, like reading cowrie shells, dominos, yarrow sticks. We might call this gradual accumulation of knowledge about specialized random patterns the beginnings of a science of divination. But science, as we know it in the Western World, requires a further step: quantification, number. And the science of divination took that step as well.

THE EVOLUTION OF YIN AND
YANG INTO THE EIGHT TRIGRAMS

At the outset, the Book of Changes was a collection of linear signs to be used as oracles. In antiquity, oracles were everywhere in use; the oldest among them confined themselves to the answers yes and no. This type of oracular pronouncement is likewise the basis of the Book of Changes. "Yes" was indicated by a simple unbroken line (−), and "No" by a broken line (- -).[9]

When we are confronted with an important choice in life, the first thing we usually try to do is simplify it. For example, we might make a list of the reasons for and a list of the reasons against such a choice. While the actual situation may be twisted

---

[9] Richard Wilhelm, *The I Ching or Book of Changes*, Bollingen Series XIX, Cary F. Baynes, trans. (Princeton: Princeton University Press, 1967), p. xlix.

in complicated ways inside us, we use such methods to try and restore some order to the situation. But it's seldom that we actually resolve anything difficult in such an overly rational way. Eventually we come down to flipping a coin—whether literally or figuratively—to determine which of two options we should honor, which path we should take. Out of such primitive sources evolved one of the most complex and wise of all oracles: the *I Ching* or *Book of Changes*.

The origins of the *I Ching* are lost in antiquity, but traditionally it is purported to have been the creation of Fu Hsi. Fu Hsi is a mythological figure who, much like Osiris in Egyptian mythology, marked the transition from barbarism to civilization. In the *Pai Hu T'ung*, written in the first century, it says of Fu Hsi:

> In the beginning there was as yet no moral nor social order. Men knew their mothers only, not their fathers. When hungry they searched for food; when satisfied, they threw away the remnants. They devoured their food hide and hair, drank the blood, and clad themselves in skins and rushes. Then came Fu Hsi and looked upward and contemplated the images in the heavens, and looked downward and contemplated the occurrences on earth. He united man and wife, regulated the five stages of change, and laid down the laws of humanity. *He devised the eight trigrams, in order to gain mastery over the world.*[10]

Here we see the origins of the philosophy of the I Ching, which in turn formed the basis of all later Chinese philosophy, especially both Taoism and Confucianism. When Fu Hsi "looked upward and contemplated the images in the heavens," he saw "*yang*, or clarity, strength, and light."[11] When he "looked downward and contemplated the occurrences on earth," he found "*yin*, or darkness, receptivity, and obscurity."[12] Everything in the universe is formed by the interaction of these two primary qualities.

---

[10] Richard Wilhelm, *I Ching*, p. 329, italics mine.
[11] Da Liu, *I Ching Numerology* (San Francisco: Harper & Row, 1979), p. 8.
[12] Da Liu, *I Ching Numerology*, p. 8.

Yang was symbolized by an unbroken line (−), Yin by a broken line (- -). Three such lines arranged one over the other were called a *trigram*. Since there were two possibilities for each line, a trigram could present any of eight different possibilities; thus the eight trigrams devised by Fu Hsi "*in order to gain mastery over the world.*" For convenience of notation here, rather than drawing lines, we will represent Yang by 1, and Yin by 0. Each of the eight trigrams can then be designated by triplets like <111>, <101>, etc. For example, <100> will represent a trigram with a yang line on the bottom, then two yin lines above.

Fu Hsi assigned each trigram an association with nature, so that all eight together described the cycle of nature. The progression discovered by Fu Hsi follows. Though several of the trigrams are repeated over the course of this story, all eight appear in this description; I've put each in bold for their initial appearance.

The sky is clear: **Ch'ien <111>**.

The wind comes: *Ch'ien*'s <111> bottom line changes: **Sun <011>**, Wind.

Wind brings heat: *Ch'ien*'s<111> middle line changes: **Li <101>**, Heat.

Heat condenses the air and clouds appear: *Ch'ien*'s top line changes: **Tui <110>**, Cloud.

Clouds are followed by rain: *Tui*'s <110> bottom line changes: **K'an <010>**, Rain.

The clear sky becomes dark: all of *Ch'ien*'s lines change: **K'un <000>**, Darkness.

The dark sky is marked by thunder: *K'un*'s <000> bottom line changes: **Chên <100>**, Thunder.

Thunder is followed by more rain: *K'un*'s <000> middle line changes: *K'an* <010>, Rain.

The Rain stops: *K'un*'s <000> top line changes: **Kên <001>**, Stop.

The Sun comes out again: *Kên*'s <001> first line changes: *Li* <101>, Heat.

Finally the sky becomes clear again: All of *K'un*'s <000> lines change: *Ch'ien* <111>.[13]

---

[13] Da Liu, *I Ching Numerology*, pp. 9–11. Bold words indicate the first mention of trigram, which is how the words are presented in Da Liu's book.

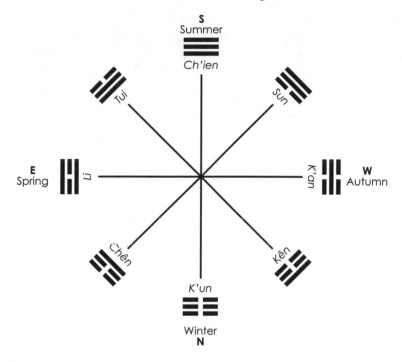

Figure 18. Sequence of Early Heaven.

Fu Hsi added further symbolic meanings for each trigram, so that each also represented not only the forces of nature, but also a member of the family.

> Father <111>, Mother <000>;
> Eldest Daughter <011>, Eldest Son <100>;
> Middle Daughter <101>, Middle Son <010>;
> Youngest Daughter <110>, and Youngest Son <001>.

Note the complementarity of the trigrams for masculine and feminine. By legend, Fu Hsi also arranged the trigrams around a circle in order to assign them number, direction, and season. This arrangement is called the "Sequence of Early Heaven." See figure 18.

The arrangement is again in terms of complementary opposites, with the primary forces—*Ch'ien* (Heaven) and *K'un*

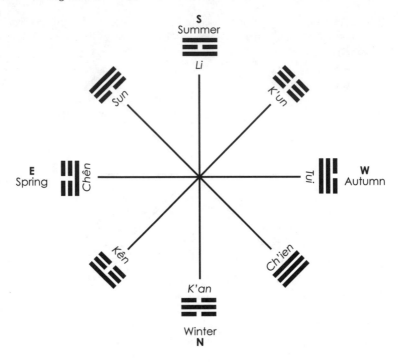

Figure 19. Sequence of Later Heaven.

(Earth) — determining the North-South axis (note that the Chinese reverse the positions for North and South). In all cases the Yang and Yin forces balance each other at every position of the complementary trigrams.

The next axis is NW/SE — *Kên* (Mountain) and *Tui* (Lake). "The wind blows from the mountain to the lake and the clouds and mists rise from the lake to the mountain."[14]

Then we have the NE/SW axis — *Chên* (Thunder) and *Sun* (Wind). When we have both wind and thunder, they magnify each other's effect.

Finally on the E/W axis we have *Li* (Fire) and *K'an* (Water). We normally think of fire and water as irreconcilable opposites,

---

[14] Richard Wilhelm, *The I Ching*, p. 266.

but in nature, both sun and water are necessary to grow a plant from a seed. All of nature is always in a process of change; both expanding, as in Fu Hsi's original description of the cycle of nature, but also contracting in the opposite direction at the same time. If we understand how things unfold, we also understand how they contract.

King Wên (1160 B.C.) developed an alternative arrangement of the eight trigrams, called the "Sequence of Later Heaven (figure 19)," which ignores the complementary pairing of trigrams in order to more clearly follow the growth cycle of nature. Beginning with Chên in the East (Spring), if we proceed clockwise along the four main compass points, we will reach Li in the South (Summer), Tui in the West (Autumn), and finally K'an in the North (Winter).

One of the ancient commentaries, apocryphally assigned to King Wên himself, explains the position of the trigrams this way:

> God comes forth in the sign of the Arousing [*Chen* in the East];
> He brings all things to completion in the Sign of the Gentle [*Sun* in the SE];
> He causes creatures to perceive one another in the sign of the Clinging (light) [*Li* in the South.]
> He causes them to serve one another in the sing of the Receptive [*K'un* in the SW];
> He gives them joy in the sign of the Joyous [*Tui* in the West];
> He battles in the sign of the Creative [*Ch'ien* in the NW];
> He toils in the sign of the Abysmal [*K'an* in the North];
> He brings them to perfection in the sign of Keeping Still [*Kên* in the NE].[15]

Considering that the trigrams have evolved over nearly five thousand years, and have formed the basis for both Confucianism and Taoism, it is not surprising that there is a huge literature on them.

---

[15] Richard Wilhelm, *The I Ching*, p. 268.
[16] Martin Gardner, "Chapter 20 — The I Ching," in his *Knotted Doughnuts and Other Mathematical Entertainments* (New York: W. H. Freeman, 1986), p. 245.

I have barely scratched the surface in the short history I have pre-sented above, and will discuss the concept of change and the Tao in the next section. But first, before we leave the trigrams, let me provide a shorthand guide to their meanings and associations. Table 3 (page 174), largely taken from puzzle-master Martin Gardner's article on the I Ching,[16] can thus serve as a shorthand when attempting to study the trigrams.

Table 3. Trigram Associations.

TRIGRAM	NAME	IMAGES	TRAITS	FAMILY	BODY	ANIMAL
111	Ch'ien	Heaven Cold	Strong Firm Creative	Father	Head	Horse
000	K'un	Earth Heat	Receptive Yielding Dark	Mother	Belly	Ox
100	Chên	Thunder Spring	Active Moving Arousing	First Son	Foot	Dragon
010	K'an	Water Moon Winter	Dangerous Difficult Enveloping	Middle Son	Ear	Pig
001	Kên	Mountain Stop	Keeping still Stubborn Unmoving	Youngest Son	Hand	Dog
011	Sun	Wind Wood	Gentle Penetrating Flexible	First Daughter	Thigh	Bird
010	Li	Fire Sun Lightning Summer	Beautiful Dependent Clinging	Middle Daughter	Eye	Pheasant
110	Tui	Lake Marsh Rain Autumn	Joyous Satisfied Complacent	Youngest Daughter	Mouth	Sheep

CHANGE, NON-CHANGE AND THE HOLOGRAPHIC UNIVERSE

In the Book of Changes a distinction is made between three kinds of change; non-change, cyclic change, and sequent change.[17]

This short summary of the scientific stance underlying the I Ching presents a profoundly modern, perhaps post-modern, model of reality. *Non-change* represents the fundamental structure of all reality, against which all change can be viewed. The world is filled with "things" which capture our attention, but reality itself is composed of emptiness, of hidden structure. It wasn't until physicists were able to descend into the atom in the 20th century that Western science realized how profoundly "empty" reality actually is. In the "Bible" of Taoism, the *Tao Te Ching*, Lao Tzu expresses this insight:

> Thirty spokes join together at one hub,
> But it is the hole that makes it operable.
> Clay is moulded into a pot,
> But it is the emptiness inside that makes it useful.
> Doors and windows are cut to make a room,
> It is the empty spaces that we use.
> *Therefore, existence is what we have,*
> *But non-existence is what we use.*[18]

In other words, reality has a structure that isn't composed of the things of the world, but of the spaces left between those things. When everything is related to everything else, it is to the spaces between that we need to look.

Cyclic change occurs everywhere against that static background. We see it most notably in the processions of the seasons. French mathematician Joseph Fourier (1768–1830) was actually able to prove that all mathematical functions, no matter

---

[17] Richard Wilhelm, *The I Ching*, p. 280.

[18] John R. Mabry, Trans. *The Little Book of the Tao Te Ching* (Boston: Element, 1995), p. 13.

[19] With the exception of some discontinuous examples that need not concern us here.

how complex,[19] can be represented by the sum of a series of periodic (cyclic or recurring) functions of different frequencies and amplitudes. These translations of complex mathematical functions into periodic functions are accordingly called *Fourier Transforms*. Without knowing it, we encountered this when we talked about the variety of brainwaves, breaking them into *delta waves* (½ to 3½ cycles/sec), *theta waves* (4 to 7 cycles/sec), *alpha waves* (8 to 13 cycles/sec), and *beta waves* (14 to 30 cycles/sec). If you've ever seen an EEG printed, you'll know that the patterns vary widely in height and width. Any person's individual EEG pattern over any substantial period of time is so complex that it will likely never be repeated by anyone in the history of the world. Yet any such pattern can be reproduced by a sum of highly regular, cyclic patterns which we chose to break into groups we call delta, theta, alpha, and beta.

It was the realization that the brain has to be able to process wave forms that led Karl Pribram to his theory of the holographic brain operating within a holographic universe. As you'll recall from our discussion of the brain, memory appears to be largely stored diffusely over the entire surface of the cortex (with more functionally centralized storage in the more ancient parts of the brain). This distributed storage is why computer programs based on the neural net model of the brain appear to learn in similar fashion to the way higher animals learn. What we didn't say then was that the mathematics that underlies this method of storage is based on Fourier Transforms.

It seems natural that the brain should have this capability when we realize that much of the information we take in from the world is in wave form: sound waves, light waves. Even the particles of matter we inhale when we eat something or smell something can, at their atomic level, be considered "wave" as much as "particle." Waves have no definition in time or space: a wave is defined simply by its amplitude and its frequency. Once begun, a wave simply continues waving endlessly. Paradoxically, even though our senses process input from the world in the form of waves, in our minds we perceive the world as made up of objects existing in time and space. Thus the brain has to have a mechanism which *transforms* (i.e., Fourier Transforms) information received in the form of waves into a form with which we can relate.

In 1947, drawing on the mathematics of Fourier Transforms, physicist Dennis Gabor proved mathematically that holographic photography was possible. By the early 1960s, with the development of laser beams, holograms became physical realities. A laser beam is a coherent light source; in other words, it's made up of waves with identical amplitudes and frequencies moving along together. To actually create a hologram, you use a prism to split a laser beam into two identical beams, then bounce each off mirrors tilted at 45 degrees, so that they reflect the two beams back to form a single beam again. If done carefully, the recombined light beam is identical to the original beam; that is, the peaks and valleys of the two beams line up exactly.

Now replace one of the mirrors with some object. The light will still be reflected off the object and recombined with the other beam, but instead of being a perfect reflection, the light waves will reflect off the nooks and crannies that make up the structure of the object. Thus, when the two beams recombine, "interference patterns" will be created. That is, the peaks and valleys of the waves won't always coincide, and they will be "out of synch" in complex ways that exactly describe the shape of the object.

What's unique about a hologram? Simply, if you record that interference pattern on a film, then shine the laser beam back through the film again, it will create a perfect, three-dimensional image of the object, since the interference pattern is, in this strange way, a perfect portrait of the object!

What is even less obvious is that a hologram thus translates between the physical world of time and space that we think we live in, and the timeless world of the unconscious (and in fact, all reality) that underlies the physical world. An object that exists in time and space is captured in an interference pattern of periodic waves that have no definition in time or space. Exposed to light, the interference pattern once more generates an object (or at least at this stage of visual holographs, a three-dimensional portrait of an object) that *does* exist in time and space. All by way of Fourier Transforms. This capability might, of course, underlie synchronicity. As Karl Pribram comments:

> Wave "numbers" can refer to densities of occurrences with respect to any number of dimensions other than or in addition to time-space. This could mean that physical

orders exist in which synchronicity rather than causality operates as a basic principle. . . . This could mean that beyond every appearance of randomness lies hidden an order that awaits discovery.[20]

In this respect, the universe, composed of an endless stream of waves — one might even call the universe a waving — exists outside of time and space. Since our brains necessarily have the ability to "collapse" those wave forms into perceived particles which do exist in time and space, it would be strange indeed if brains did not receive and translate information that can't be expressed in terms of physical cause-and-effect. Everything in reality connects to everything else through the intermingling of wave forms. Relationships are thus largely *acausal*; causality is the exception, not the rule.

But these realizations are already contained within the philosophy that underlies the I Ching. The founder of Taoism, Lao Tzu, lived in the sixth century B.C. and was contemporary with, but older than Confucius.[21] Interestingly, this is roughly the same time as when Plato and Aristotle lived in Greece, and Lao Tzu and Confucius were as different in their views of reality as were Plato and Aristotle. Over-simplifying their positions a bit, we might say that Confucius and Aristotle believed in the "things" of the world, while Lao Tzu and Plato believed in a deeper reality that underlay the "thousand things" (a Chinese phrase for the multiplicity of the things of the world). Here's a story about the difference between Confucius and Lao Tzu in which Lao Tzu presents a view of reality much like I have presented in this book.

One day Confucius came to see Lao Tzu and saw him sitting utterly motionless. He withdrew and waited, then presented himself once more and asked Lao Tzu where he had been. Lao Tzu answered, "I had voyaged to the World's Beginning." When Confucius asked him what he meant by that, Lao Tzu answered, "The mind is darkened by what it learns there and cannot under-

---

[20] Karl Pribram, "The Brain," in Alberto Villoldo and Ken Dychtwald, eds., *Millennium: Glimpses into the 21st Century* (Los Angeles: J. P. Tarcher, 1981), p. 102.
[21] Ch'u Chai, *The Story of Chinese Philosophy*, pp. 69–70.

stand; the lips are folded and cannot speak. But I will try to embody for you some semblance of what I saw. I saw Yin, the Female Energy, in its motionless grandeur. I saw Yang, the Male energy, rampant in its fiery vigour. The motionless grandeur came up out of the earth; the fiery vigour burst out from heaven. The two penetrated one another, were inextricably blended and from their union the things of the world were born."[22]

If we think of Yin and Yang as two complementary positions, much like the peaks and the valleys of wave forms, we can see this as a description of how all reality is made up of the union of such timeless, nonphysical qualities.

CONSULTING THE I CHING

The first people to use the *Changes* [i.e., the *Book of Changes* or *I Ching*] were priestly diviners serving the feudal lords of the Bronze Age Zhou Dynasty in China, sometime between about 1000 and 500 B.C.[23]

Though we don't know exactly when the *I Ching* itself evolved out of the ancient system of the trigrams, it is likely to have been about 3,000 years ago, since it already had a substantial history before extensive additions were made by Confucius and his followers, probably in the sixth century B.C. At some point in the perhaps two thousand years between the first appearance of Fu Hsi's trigrams and the first compilation of wisdom and divination known as the Book of Changes, two trigrams were combined into a single hexagram, which multiplied the possibilities from eight to sixty-four. We have already said the concept of change is embedded in the philosophical underpinning of the *I Ching*. Thus each of the sixty-four hexagrams is viewed, not as a static condition, but as a force moving from past to future. Individual lines can be not only yin or yang, but also static or mov-

---

[22] Arthur Waley, *Three Ways of Thought in Ancient China* (Garden City, NY: Doubleday/Anchor Books, 1939), p. 16.
[23] Greg Whincup, *Rediscovering the I Ching* (Garden City, NY: Doubleday, 1986), p. 1. Brackets mine.

ing (more on this later), which increased the sixty-four possibilities represented by hexagrams to 4,096, when the readings for the individual lines are also considered. And, since those possibilities obviously have different shadings dependent on the question being asked, the *I Ching* can seem limitless in its capacity for providing oracular wisdom.

There are many translations of the I Ching, and many additional versions which, while not true translations from the original, are "translations" from the translations to make the text more accessible for various audiences. The first Western translation was by James Legge,[24] but undoubtedly the best known and most used is the Richard Wilhelm translation, further translated from German into English by Cary F. Baynes.[25] This version is comparable in its beauty to the King James version of the Bible. Other well-known English translations include those by John Blofeld[26] and Thomas Cleary.[27] One recent translation of a translation (based on the Legge translation) that I like very much is Christopher Markert's *I Ching: The No. 1 Success Formula.*[28] I can only assume the atrocious and misleading subtitle is due to a marketing editor, as this is a thoughtful rendering of the I Ching for a modern reader. And for a number of years, I've used a computer version, developed by R. K Thompson, with a fine original translation by J. L. Schroeder.[29]

I would suggest that the reader buy a copy of the Wilhelm/Baynes version, which even in an attractive hardbound edition, is not expensive due to its wide availability. It provides not only a beautiful translation of the I Ching itself, but extensive historical and interpretive material, as well as a famous foreword by C. G. Jung in which he presents the *I Ching* as an example of his principle of synchronicity.

---

[24] James Legge, *I Ching: The Sacred Books of China: The Book of Changes* (Dover, 1975). Among many other editions of this translation.

[25] Richard Wilhelm, *The I Ching or Book of Changes,* Bollingen Series XIX, Cary F. Baynes, trans. (Princeton: Princeton University Press, 1967).

[26] John Blofeld, *The I Ching (The Book of Changes)* (London: George Allen & Unwin, 1965). Among many other editions of this book.

[27] Thomas Cleary, *I Ching: The Book of Changes* (Boston: Shambhala, 1986). Among other editions of this translation.

[28] Christopher Markert, *I Ching: The No. 1 Success Formula* (London: Aquarian Press, 1986). A particular version of the book.

[29] J. L. Schroeder, trans., R. K. Thompson, programmer, *Chou I: The Change of Chou: A Computer Version of the I Ching* (R. K. Thompson, 1995).

Coins	Value	Line	Symbol
3 Tails	6 (2 + 2 + 2)	Moving Yin	-x-
2 Tails, 1 Head	7 (2 + 2 + 3)	Static Yang	—
2 Heads, 1 Tail	8 (3 + 3 + 2)	Static Yin	- -
3 Heads	9 (3 + 3 + 3)	Moving Yang	-o-

Figure. 20. Coin Method to Consult the I Ching.

In all of its many versions, the *I Ching* contains descriptions of the 64 hexagrams, which provide primary information on the question asked, plus further commentaries on any of the six lines of the hexagram which are *moving*. The universe, as seen by the *I Ching*, is composed of yin and yang, but a yin line may be in the process of changing into a yang line, or vice versa. Such lines are known as *old yin* and *old yang* or more simply as *moving lines*.

Traditionally, one determined the six lines of the hexagram by dividing 49 yarrow stalks into two piles, then going through a prescribed and lengthy procedure based on *modulo 4* arithmetic.[30] More commonly in the Western world, the lines are determined by throwing three coins (often special Chinese coins to fit the feeling of the *I Ching*, but any coins will do) six times. I'll describe that procedure here.

No matter what type of coins you use, decide in advance which side is *heads* and which is *tails*. In determining what line you derive from casting the coins, a head is considered yang and assigned a value of 3; a tail is considered yin and assigned a value of 2. Shake the three coins in your hand, then drop them in front of you. The type of line is determined as shown in figure 20.

This isn't as confusing as it sounds. Let's describe it a couple of other ways. First, notice that the even numbers are all yin, whether we're discussing 2 for an individual coin, 6 for a moving yin line, or 8 for a static yin line. Similarly the odd numbers are all yang, whether 3 for a single coin, 7 for a static yang line,

---

[30] Modulo 4 arithmetic simply means the remainder left from a number when divided by 4. 5 modulo 4 would be 1; 38 modulo 4 would be 2, and so forth.

or 9 for a moving yang line. So if you can remember that heads are 3 (odd, yang) and tails are 2 (even, yin), you'll quickly get it.

Another way to think of the results is that if you have three coins all facing the same way, that's too much of that quality, so the line is beginning to change into its opposite. Thus 3 heads are too much yang, so a moving yang line; 3 tails too much yin, so a moving yin line. A mix of two of one kind and one of another is just right and the type of line is determined by the coin that doesn't match. That is, 2 heads and 1 tail is determined by the tail, so it's a yin line—a static yin line; 2 tails and 1 head is determined by the head, so it's a static yang line.

Still another simple way is to remember our earlier notation of "1" for a yang line (heads) and "0" for a yin line (tails). It's a lot easier to add 0's and 1's. If you get "0", it's a moving yin line (remember, too much yin); a "2" is a static yin line. A "1" is a static yang line and "3" a moving yang line (too much yang). Or simply keep a little chart like the one above in front of you until this is all clear in your memory.

As you determine the first line, draw it on a piece of paper, leaving a little room to its left. The second line goes above the first, and you continue until you have the six lines that make up a hexagram. If there are any moving lines (and there will be roughly four out of five times you consult the *I Ching*), you want to expand your original drawing as follows:

18–Decay		59–The Joyous
—	—	—
- -	-x-	—
- -	- -	- -
—	-o-	- -
—	—	—
- -	- -	- -
	3,5	

I've drawn a sample throw in the middle. As you can see, it has a moving yang line third from the bottom, and a moving yin line fifth from the bottom. That's why I wrote 3,5 below the hexagram. On the left, I've shown the hexagram before the moving lines change into their opposite; i.e., the moving yang is simply a yang line, the moving yin a simple static yin line. On the right I've done the same thing, except that this time the moving yang has moved on and become a yin line, the moving yin has become a yang line. Again this will take a little getting used to, but it soon becomes straightforward.

Finally, I've used the following chart (see Table 4), which is included in all versions of the *I Ching*, to look up what hexagram corresponds to these lines, and I've written them above the hexagrams on the left and right (i.e., "18" and "59"). In order for the chart to show all 64 hexagrams in the smallest space, it lists the bottom trigram on the left and the top trigram along the top of the chart. You just match the right two trigrams and you have the number for the hexagram. For space considerations, I've used the same shorthand of "1" for yang lines and "0" for yin lines that I used earlier in this chapter. The hexagram on the left is thus composed of <011> below and <001> above. The hexagram on the right is <010> below and <011> above.

Table 4. The Hexagram from the Upper and Lower Trigrams.

UPPER→ LOWER↓	CH'IEN <111>	CHÊN <100>	K'AN <010>	KÊN <001>	K'UN <000>	SUN <011>	LI <101>	TUI <110>
Ch'ien <111>	1	34	5	26	11	9	14	43
Chên <100>	25	51	3	27	24	42	21	17
K'an <010>	6	40	29	4	7	59	64	47
Kên <001>	33	62	39	52	15	53	56	31
K'un <000>	12	16	8	23	2	20	35	45
Sun <011>	44	32	48	18	46	57	50	28
Li <101>	13	55	63	22	36	37	30	49
Tui <110>	10	54	60	41	19	61	38	58

[31] Richard Wilhelm, *The I Ching or Book of Changes*, pp. 75–78.

Once you know the appropriate hexagram, you turn to the text of the *I Ching*. The structure of most translations are similar; we'll use Wilhelm in this description. All of the quotations from the I Ching in the next few pages are from William's translation.[31] There is a drawing of the hexagram, with the two trigrams identified. A short summary explains how the symbolic meaning of the hexagram has been derived from the two trigrams. In our example, Hexagram 18 is "*Ku*: Work on What Has Been Spoiled (Decay)," and the summary says that "the Chinese character *Ku* represents a bowl in whose contents worms are breeding. . . . The meaning of the hexagram is not simply 'what has been spoiled' but 'work on what has been spoiled.'"

So this hexagram talks about a situation where one needs to work on unresolved issues. In psychological terms, it often deals with unresolved childhood issues with one's parents. But it can be almost any situation where work remains to be done. The Judgement follows, which is the capsule, poetic summary of the situation. In this case:

> "*Work on what has been spoiled*
> Has supreme success.
> It further one to cross the great water.
> Before the starting point, three days.
> After the starting point, three days."

An amplification of what this "judgment" implies follows. These amplifications are considered to have been added by Confucius or his followers. Though the "judgment" is normally symbolic," it is surprising how often it fits literally. For example, though "it furthers one to cross the great water" normally implies being willing to make a major transition, often it literally means taking a trip over the ocean. Again "before the starting point, three days, after the starting point, three days" implies taking time to think something through carefully before one proceeds, then thinking over the results afterward, but often "three days" actually means "three days."

"The Image" follows "The Judgment." Nothing demonstrates more clearly that the *I Ching* has come out of a deep inner place, as "the image" is an attempt to express a concept like "decay" in symbolic terms. Here it says that:

"The wind blows low on the mountain:
The image of *Decay*.
Thus the superior man stirs up the people
And strengthens their spirit."

As with the "judgment" an amplification follows. Here it says "when the wind blows low on the mountain, it is thrown back and spoils the vegetation. This contains a challenge to improvement. . . ." The phrase "superior man" occurs often in the *I Ching* and implies a sage, a person who has completed his inner journey, who follows the *tao*. Though translated as "man" it actually has no gender and actually implies simply a "superior person."

Following "The Image" are the glosses on the individual moving lines. These are important to consider. Though they are always consistent with the general situation of the hexagram, they may either amplify or reverse the general reading of the hexagram. In our example, the moving lines are 3 and 5. The text for 3 is "setting right what has been spoiled by a father. There will be little remorse. No great blame." And 5 reads "setting right what has been spoiled by the father. One meets with praise."

So both lines mention father issues. What this means varies with the context of the person and the situation, but let me turn to the same lines in Markert's modern version for his interpretation. For those same two lines, he says, "If he is faced with rigid habits or demanding traditions, he knows that it would be futile to revolt against them. Instead he proceeds with subtlety and intelligence to replace the obsolete order with a more appropriate one." And for line 5, "He reviews the obsolete standards and creates a new order. If he handles the situation intelligently, he will be praised by all involved." He thus considers "father issues" as dealing with traditions or standards, a reasonable conclusion, but not necessarily what *you* might decide for your particular situation. It is always necessary to reach your own conclusions as to what these highly symbolic readings mean with respect to your life and the problem that has prompted you to consult the *I Ching*.

Finally you need to consider the second hexagram: "59–Dispersion (Dissolution)," in our case. Think of the second hexagram not as a prediction of the future, but as that which is emerging out of the current situation if things remain the same.

Even those who initially consult the *I Ching* with skepticism, tend to come away impressed. Their attitude coming in is often that "the text is so ambiguous that, no matter what hexagrams are selected, it is always possible to interpret them so that they seem to apply to the question."[32] But if the *I Ching* is consulted on a matter of real concern to the person, the answers tend to be so apt that this reductionist explanation is hard to maintain. In my own experience, I have never received one of the highly positive hexagrams (such as "11–Peace," "14–Possession in Great Measure," "19–Approach," "42–Increase," "55–Abundance") in a genuinely dark period of my life (except, of course, with a moving line that mediated the answer). And I have never received one of the darker hexagrams ("12–Standstill," "29–The Abysmal," "36–Darkening of the Light," "47–Oppression") except when I was struggling with difficult issues. Thus, though it is true that, as with any oracle, sometimes the meaning of the hexagram is unclear, the general direction is always to the point. And, as we have explained in our discussion of synchronicity (which underlies all oracles), the more emotional energy you have invested in the situation, the more likely the answer is to be clear and direct.

• • •

The *I Ching* is perhaps the wisest of all oracles. It can be read simply as a book of wisdom, much as one would read a profound religious or philosophic book, without ever making use of it as a divinatory tool. Many scholars feel more comfortable approaching it this way. But it evolved out of simpler divinatory methods, and it is as a method of divination that it has lasted over so many thousands of years. It is as wise today as when Confucius and Lao Tzu learned from it twenty-five hundred years ago.

---

[32] Martin Gardner, *Knotted Doughnuts and Other Mathematical Entertainments,* p. 254.

AFTERWORD

What does the fine chaff say to the wind?
Each wound is an eye; see me
and you shall be healed. Your laughter is the river
on fire, your touch is the wet stones
shining in the empty arms of water,
your dream is the shadow of the sun,
awkward and disobedient in the fields
of this summer's evening between worlds;
and your anguish moves the stars in their lonely closet
to sing the long dark songs we love.

We are here now, together. These wings in the distance like
lips waking, these blue eyelids opening beneath the horizon, these are
voices from the well of the future
no longer frightened to be born. This breathing
you hear in the wind all around you is a gift
freely given by the healing angels,
the angels of the wheat.
—Richard Messer[1]

This book began with the curious premise that everything significant in our lives emerges, not from the world outside, but from the inside-out. This may have sounded strange at first, but I hope that by now you've come to regard it simply as a straightforward model of reality.

The structure and operation of the brain helps explain why this is so. As described in chapter 3, the brain might better be considered as three brains—the *reptile brain*, the *mammal brain*, and the *human brain*—each of which developed at vastly different points in time. Though all three brains are interconnected,

---

[1] Richard Messer, unpublished poem, given to author in e-mail communication.

the reptile and mammal brains largely function without inter-ference from the human brain. Here the analogy to the com-puter model of the brain helps us understand how they relate (though it's important to remember that this computer model is a vastly over-simplified model). There are behavioral "pro-grams" stored within the structure of the reptile and human brain, programs that go back largely unchanged to a time long before humans were even a glimpse on the horizon. When we get "territorial" and react instinctively to "protect our turf," a program in the reptile brain is kicking in. When we try to find our place in the "pecking order" at work, we draw on knowl-edge hidden in the mammal brain. Most of our wants and needs, thoughts and behaviors, are triggered by programs that are millions, if not hundreds of millions, of years old.

This isn't to say that our reactions are identical to the behav-ior of a crocodile protecting its territory, or a chimp grooming another chimp, but at their core, our reactions are more similar than we would like to believe. Evolution, by its very definition, is a slow process. Either we can regard this connection to sup-posed "lower animals" with indignation, or we can accept that we are all bound together within a web of life that encompasses all creatures in all times. When I read Lorenz' story about the jackdaw trying to "court" him by feeding him worms, I was charmed and thought immediately of times when I had tried to come up with just the right present for a girl I was dating (though I admit that I never came up with worms). And what parent can't appreciate the jackdaws instinctively rushing to de-fend against anything that might attack their children. I think it's better to realize how much we share with other animals than to keep stressing how unique we are.

Our uniqueness lies in that human brain that surrounds the reptile and mammal brains. Gerald Edelman's model of Neural Darwinism gives us an idea of how all these operate together in our lives. Within the brain's structure we have approximately *one hundred billion* neurons divided into perhaps *one hundred mil-lion* neuron groups. Each of those groups might be considered as a program storing some tiny portion of behavior. At birth we se-lect about a million of those groups as a *primary repertoire*. That leaves 99 percent of the neuron groups unused at birth. Clearly there are enough possible stored behaviors to deal, at least broadly, with almost anything in human experience, but also clearly the million neuron groups in the primary repertoire are hardly enough to account for all our behaviors.

But development doesn't stop at birth: as we experience the world during our life (especially our early life), the primary repertoire (and quite possibly neuron groups not originally selected in the primary repertoire) is connected and reconnected in myriads of different ways specific to our life experience.

And even that isn't all. Within the human brain, it appears that much of our learned behavior is stored diffusely throughout the entire structure of the brain. Neural nets provide a possible model of how memories might come into existence. As an illustration of how neural nets form, I gave an example of how we arrive at a consensus during a town meeting. At this point, it isn't yet clear exactly how this process operates in the brain, though neurophysiologist and psychologist Karl Pribram speculates that holographic memories are formed within the dendritic connections of the brain. Because much of the information received by our brains is in waves, our brains have hard-wired programs that perform Fourier transforms, which convert the diffuse wave patterns into structured patterns.

This is exactly the same process performed by holograms. And, since the entire universe is made up neither of particles nor waves, but rather of particle/waves, this ability of our brains would explain how we could not only access information stored deep within the brain's structure over millennia, but also could bypass space-time limitations. This holographic theory, which appears to be supported by what we know of the brain's structure, provides at least a preliminary model to explain how dreams can provide information not known to the dreamer, how synchronicity can connect events acausally, how divinatory devices, like the I Ching, can provide information not available to consciousness.

GATEWAYS AND RITUALS

Most of this book dealt with specific "gateways" through which we are able to access "inside" information. Dreams are the method *par excellence*, as evolution has already provided us with this structure for accessing otherwise unobtainable information. I explained that dreams begin to develop in the age of the dinosaurs almost a quarter of a billion years ago and were fully developed 65 millions years ago. From then until now, all birds and mammals (and probably reptiles) have dreamt each night. That is a very long time. Clearly dreams serve a significant function.

I described rituals, techniques to help remember, honor, and interpret dreams. If you do no more than begin to keep a dream journal, you will have taken a major step toward creating harmony between inner and outer, a harmony that will be reflected in the way you live your life.

Another, less well-known gateway into the inner world is through synchronicity. As with dreams, synchronicities appear in our lives whether we pay attention to them or not. As with all things, however, becoming conscious makes all the difference in the world. Synchronicity appears to be a natural extension of two principles: *saliency* and *synchrony*. The world is filled with sights, and sounds, and smells, and other data not interpretable by our senses. Whether this data is interpreted as "noise" or "meaning" depends entirely on the circumstances, much like a key is only useful when the proper lock is found. This is *saliency*. When the proper information is received by more than one person, for example, a *synchrony* forms between them. A simple conversation, for example, when videotaped and observed at slower speeds, appears as a synchronous dance. Information is coming to us all the time: some we interpret as noise, some as meaningful. We are dancing to the music of the universe. Synchronicities are the most obvious manifestation of that dance.

Not only is our evolutionary history stored within the structure of our brains, it is also stored within the structure of our bodies in energy centers called *chakras*. Though chakras are ignored by traditional Western science, chakras have been known to most cultures throughout history. The difficulty in gaining acceptance for chakras in our Western culture is that they are *psychoid* structures (to use Jung's term); that is, they are both body and psyche. In the body, they are located at sites that correspond to the major glands; as psyche, they are experienced in our developmental cycle, which mirrors the entire evolutionary history of the universe. While that may seem too grand to deal with, we can become aware of chakras through our breathing, a unique function that is under the control of both our sympathetic and parasympathetic systems. For example, our bodies keep us breathing without any effort on our part, yet we can take conscious control of our breathing any time we like.

This unique aspect of breathing leads to another major gateway to our inner life—*meditation*. Though we don't know if any animals other than human beings meditate, we do know that meditation is a very ancient human ritual. I presented ways to meditate, with an emphasis on the Zen technique of simply observing the breath until we become one with it. I also presented a personally developed technique of breathing through the chakras, which is especially powerful. Aids to meditation were described, including light and sound *mind machines*, as well as numerous examples of music that help induce altered states of consciousness.

In an altered state of consciousness, we are capable of speaking for the gods—accessing information that is seemingly unavailable to anyone. There is a long history of such oracular techniques, with the most famous being the Oracle at Delphi. But this ability is not limited to far-off places and times; a technique discovered by C. G. Jung called *active imagination* allows us to turn to deeper powers within us to obtain information.

Another ancient oracle is the *I Ching*, a volume of wisdom that can be consulted by combining chance with a predefined structure. Because the *I Ching* is such a powerful gateway available to all, I described it at some length, explaining its history and structure, as well as the actual mechanics of consulting it.

If, by now, all I've said sounds natural, even commonplace, this book will have served its purpose. But don't let that mislead you; this is a revolutionary view of reality, one that might restore meaning to the world! It has, unfortunately become commonplace for educated people, thinking themselves modern and scientific, to assume that the world is the product of chance, and life is without meaning. But really this is an outmoded view of the world based not only on out-of-date science, but also on an undervaluation of our own abilities. Each of us routinely makes use of the knowledge and power contained within us, but we rarely take that into account in our philosophy of life.

People who accept that life has meaning, and that we have access to that meaning from within, lives a much different life than one who, like 17th-century philosopher Thomas Hobbes, regards life as "solitary, poor, nasty, brutish, and short." The world is strange and beautiful and each of us is not only contained within that world, but also contains that world within us.

BIBLIOGRAPHY

Adams, Richard. *Watership Down.* New York: MacMillan, 1972.

Allman, William F. *Apprentices of Wonder: Inside the Neural Network Revolution.* New York: Bantam, 1989.

American Heritage Dictionary, 2nd college ed. Boston: Houghton Mifflin, 1991.

American Heritage Talking Dictionary. New York: Learning Company, 1997.

Anderson, James A. and Edward Rosenfeld, eds. *Neurocomputing: Foundations of Research.* Cambridge, MA: MIT Press, 1988.

Barnet, Sylvan, Morton Berman, William Burton, eds. *Eight Great Tragedies.* J. T. Sheppard, trans. New York: Mentor, 1957.

Bean, Orson. *Me and the Orgone.* New York: St. Martin's Press, 1971.

Benson, Herbert. *The Relaxation Response.* New York: Morrow, 1975.

Blofeld, John. *The I Ching (The Book of Changes).* London: George Allen & Unwin, 1965.

Boa, Frank and Marie-Louise von Franz: *The Way of the Dream Interpretations with Marie Louise von Franz.* Boston: Shambhala, 1999.

Borges, Jorge Luis. *Other Inquisitions: 1937–1952.* New York: Washington Square Press, 1966.

Brain/Mind Bulletin. "Gray's Theory Incorporates Earlier Evolutionary Model of 'Triune Brain,'" March 29, 1982.

Bullfinch, Thomas. *Age of Fable or Beauties of Mythology.* New York: Heritage Press, 1942.

Carrington, Patricia. *Freedom in Meditation.* Garden City, NY: Anchor, 1978.

Chai, Ch'u. *The Story of Chinese Philosophy.* New York: Washington Square Press, 1964.

Cleary, Thomas. *I Ching: The Book of Changes.* Boston: Shambhala, 1986.

Combs, Allan and Mark Holland. *Synchronicity: Science, Myth, and the Trickster.* New York: Paragon House, 1990.

Crick, Francis. *What Mad Pursuit: A Personal View of Scientific Discovery.* New York: Basic Books, 1988.

Crick, Francis, and Graeme Mitchison. "The Function of Dream Sleep," in *Nature* 312, 1983.

————. "REM Sleep and Neural Nets," *Journal of Mind and Behavior,* vol. 7, 1986.

Diamond, Edwin. *The Science of Dreams.* London: Eyre & Spottiswoode, 1962.

Dickinson, Peter. *Chance, Luck and Destiny.* Boston: Little, Brown, 1976.

Edelman, Gerald M. *Neural Darwinism.* New York: Basic Books, 1987.

Evans-Wentz, W. Y., ed. *The Tibetan Book of the Dead,* London: Oxford University Press, 1974.

Ferguson, Marilyn. *The Brain Revolution.* New York: Taplinger, 1973.

Feynman, Richard. *The Character of Physical Law.* Cambridge: MIT Press, 1965.

Flournoy, Théodore. *From India to the Planet Mars: A Case of Multiple Personality with Imaginary Languages.* Princeton: Princeton University Press, 1994.

Frye, Northrup, ed. *Selected Poetry and Prose of William Blake.* New York: Modern Library, 1953.

Gardner, Martin. *Knotted Doughnuts and Other Mathematical Entertainments.* New York: W. H. Freeman, 1986.

Goldstein, Rebecca. *The Mind-Body Problem.* New York: Random House, 1983.

Grote, George. *A History of Greece.* London: John Murray, 1854. Website: www.elibrary/com/s/edumark, April 2000.

Gutheil, Emil A. *The Handbook of Dream Analysis.* New York: Washington Square Press, 1970.

Hall, Edward T. *Beyond Culture.* Garden City, NY: Anchor Books, 1977.

————. *The Hidden Dimension.* Garden City, NY: Anchor Books, 1969.

Hampden-Turner, Charles. *Maps of the Mind.* New York: MacMillan, 1981.

Hirai, Tomio. *Zen and the Mind: Scientific Approach to Zen Practice.* Tokyo: Japan Publications, 1978.

Hobson, J. Allan. *The Dreaming Brain*. New York: Basic Books, 1988.

Holton, Gerald. *Thematic Origins of Scientific Thought*. Cambridge, MA: Harvard University Press, 1973.

Hutchison, Michael. *Megabrain*. New York: Ballantine, 1986.

Jaffé, Aniela. *Apparitions and Precognition*. New Hyde Park, NY: University Books, 1963.

———. *From the Life and Work of C. G. Jung*. R. F. C. Hull and Murray Stein, trans. Einsiedeln, Switzerland: Daimon Verlag, 1989.

James, William. *The Principles of Psychology*, vol. 1. New York: Henry Holt, 1890; reprint Dover, 1950.

———. *Psychology (Brief Course)*. New York: Henry Holt, 1890.

Jauch, J. M. *Are Quanta Real?* Bloomington: Indiana University Press, 1973.

Jeannerod, Marc. *The Brain Machine: The Development of Neurophysiological Thought*. Cambridge, MA: Harvard University Press, 1985.

Johari, Harish. *Chakras: Energy Centers of Transformation*. Rochester VT: Destiny, 1987.

Jowett, Benjamin, trans. *Dialogues of Plato*. New York: Washington Square Press, 1950.

Jung, C. G. *Two Essays on Analytical Psychology:* Collected Works vol. 7, R. F. C. Hull, trans. Bollingen Series XX. Princeton: Princeton University Press, 2nd ed. 1953/1966.

———. *The Structure and Dynamics of the Psyche:* Collected Works vol. 8, R. F. C. Hull, trans. Bollingen Series XX. Princeton: Princeton University Press, 1969.

———. *Psychology and Religion: West and East:* Collected Works, vol. 11, R. F. C. Hull, trans. Bollingen Series XX. Princeton: Princeton University Press, 2nd edition, 1969.

———. *Psychology and Alchemy:* Collected Works, vol. 12, R. F. C. Hull, trans. Bollingen Series XX. Princeton: Princeton University Press, 2nd ed., 1968.

———. *The Practice of Psychotherapy:* Collected Works, vol. 16, R. F. C. Hull, trans. Bollingen Series XX. Princeton: Princeton University Press, 1954.

———. ed., *Man and His Symbols*. New York: Anchor, Doubleday, 1964.

————. *Memories, Dreams, Reflections,* New York: Pantheon, revised ed., 1973.

Kaster, Joseph, trans. and ed. *Wings of the Falcon: Life and Thought of Ancient Egypt.* New York: Holt, Rinehart & Winston, 1968.

Krippner, Stanley, ed. *Dreamtime & Dreamwork: Decoding the Language of the Night.* New York: Tarcher/Putnam, 1990.

Krippner, Stanley and Patrick Welch. *Spiritual Dimensions of Healing: From Native Shamanism to Contemporary Health Care.* New York: Irvington Publishers, 1992.

Krishna, Gopi. *Kundalini: The Evolutionary Energy in Man.* Boston: Shambhala, 1971.

Legge, James. *I Ching: The Sacred Books of China: The Book of Changes.* New York: Dover, 1975.

LeShan, Lawrence. *The Medium, the Mystic, and the Physicist.* New York: Viking, 1974.

Liu, Da. *I Ching Numerology.* San Francisco: Harper & Row, 1979.

Lockley, Ronald. *The Private Life of a Rabbit: An Account of the Life History and Social Behavior of the Wild Rabbit.* London: Andre Deutsch, 1965.

Lorenz, Konrad. *King Solomon's Ring.* New York: Time Incorporated, 1952.

Mabry, John R., trans. *The Little Book of the Tao Te Ching.* Boston: Element, 1995.

Mansfield, Victor. *Synchronicity, Science and Soul-Making.* Chicago: Open Court, 1995.

Markert, Christopher. *I Ching: The No. 1 Success Formula.* London: Aquarian Press, 1986.

McGuire, William, ed. *C. G. Jung Speaking: Interviews and Encounters.* R. F. C. Hull and Ralph Manheim, trans. Bollingen Series XCVII. Princeton: Princeton University Press, 1977.

Metzner, Ralph. *Know Your Type: Maps of Identity.* Garden City, NY: Anchor, 1979.

Milton, Ronald. "On the Morning of Christ's Nativity," in *The Milton Reading Room.* www.dartmouth.edul~milton. April 2000.

Moffitt, Alan. "The Creation of Self in Dreaming and Waking," in *Psychological Perspectives,* Issue 30. Los Angeles: C. G. Jung Institute, 1994.

Moffitt, Alan, M. Kramer and R. Hoffman, eds. *The Functions of Dreaming*. Albany: State University of New York Press, 1993.

Mookerjee, Ajit. *Kundalini: The Arousal of Inner Energy*. Rochester, VT: Destiny, 1982.

Murphy, William. *The Future of the Body*. New York: J. P. Tarcher/Putnam, 1992.

Oppenheim, A. Leo. "The Interpretation of Dreams in the Ancient Near East with a Translation of an Assyrian Dream-Book," in *Transactions of the American Philosophical Society* 46, pt. 3, 1956.

Peat, F. David. *Synchronicity: The Bridge between Mind and Matter*. New York: Bantam, 1987.

Pribram, Karl. "Holographic Memory: Karl Pribram Interviewed by Daniel Goleman," in *Psychology Today*. Feb. 1979, no. 9.

Progoff, Ira. *Jung, Synchronicity, and Human Destiny*. New York: Dell, 1973.

Reed, Henry. "The Art of Remembering Dreams," in *Quadrant,* Summer, 1996.

———. "Intimacy and Psi: A Initial Exploration," in *Journal for the American Society for Psychical Research,* 88, Oct. 1994.

Reich, Wilhelm. *Character Analysis,* New York: Touchstone/Simon & Schuster, 3rd ed., 1972.

———. *The Function of the Orgasm*. New York: Touchstone/Simon & Schuster, 1973.

Richter, Jean Paul. *The Notebooks of Leonardo da Vinci,* 2 vols. New York: Dover Publications, 1970.

Robertson, Robin. *Beginner's Guide to Jungian Psychology*. York Beach, ME: Nicolas-Hays, 1992.

———. *Your Shadow*. Virginia Beach: A.R.E. Press, 1997.

Robinson, James M. (ed.) *The Nag Hammadi Library*. San Francisco: HarperSanFrancisco, 1988.

Rose, Steven. *The Conscious Brain*. New York: Vintage Books, 1976.

Rossi, Ernest Lawrence. *Dreams and the Growth of Personality,* 2nd edition. New York: Brunner/Mazel, 1972/1985.

Russo, Richard A. *Dreams are Wiser than Men*. Berkeley: North Atlantic Books, 1987.

Sagan, Carl. *The Dragons of Eden: Speculations of the Evolution of Human Intelligence*. New York: Ballantine Books, 1977.

Schroeder, J. L., trans. and R. K. Thompson, programmer. *Chou I: The Change of Chou: A Computer Version of the I Ching.* Computer Shareware program, R. K. Thompson, 1995.

Schwartz, Tony. *What Really Matters.* New York: Bantam Books, 1995.

Sekida, Katsuki. *Zen Training: Methods and Philosophy.* New York: John Winterhill, 1975.

Shattock, E. H. *An Experiment in Mindfulness.* New York: E. P. Dutton, 1960.

Snow, C. P. *Public Affairs.* New York: Charles Scribner's Sons, 1971.

Sogyal, Rinpoche. *Tibetan Book of Living and Dying.* New York: HarperCollins, 1992.

Spiegelman, J. Marvin and Mokusen Miyuki. *Buddhism and Jungian Psychology.* Phoenix, AZ: New Falcon Press, 1985.

Suzuki, D. T. *Manual of Zen Buddhism.* London: Rider, 1950.

Sulis, William F. Unpublished paper for UNESCO conference, 1999.

Untermeyer, Louis, ed. *Modern American & Modern British Poetry.* New York: Harcourt, Brace & World, 1955.

Van de Castle, Robert L. *Our Dreaming Mind.* New York: Ballantine Books, 1994.

van de Wetering, Janwillem. *The Empty Mirror: Experiences in a Japanese Zen Monastery.* Boston: Houghton Mifflin, 1974.

————. *A Glimpse of Nothingness.* London: Routledge & Kegan Paul, 1975.

Villoldo, Alberto and Ken Dychtwald, eds. *Millennium: Glimpses into the 21st Century.* Los Angeles: J. P. Tarcher, 1981.

von Franz, Marie-Louise. *C. G. Jung: His Myth in Our Time.* New York: G. P. Putnam's Sons, 1975.

————. *On Divination and Synchronicity: The Psychology of Meaningful Coincidence.* Toronto: Inner City Books, 1980.

————. *Time: Rhythm and Repose.* New York: Thames and Hudson, 1978.

Voss, Sarah. *What Number Is God?: Metaphors, Metaphysics, Metamathematics, and the Nature of Things.* Albany: SUNY Press, 1995.

Waley, Arthur. *Three Ways of Thought in Ancient China.* Garden City, NY: Doubleday/Anchor Books, 1939.

Walker, Benjamin. *The Encyclopedia of the Occult, the Esoteric, and the Supernatural.* New York: Scarborough Book/Stein & Day, 1980.

Waters, Frank. *The Book of the Hopi.* New York: Viking Press, 1963.

Wheeler, John A., K. S. Thorne and C. Misner. *Gravitation.* San Francisco: W. H. Freeman, 1973.

Whincup, Greg. *Rediscovering the I Ching.* Garden City, NY: Doubleday, 1986.

Whitehead, Alfred North. *The Concept of Nature.* Cambridge: Cambridge University Press, 1983.

Wilhelm, Richard and Cary F. Baynes, trans. *The I Ching or Book of Changes.* Bollingen Series XIX, Princeton: Princeton University Press, 1967.

Zukav, Gary. "What is the Soul?" in *Life Magazine,* December 1997.

———. *The Dancing Wu Li Masters.* New York: Bantam, 1979.

INDEX

Robin Robertson is a psychologist, magician, mathematician, and writer, who has spent a lifetime bridging the worlds of science, psychology and the arts. He has written ten books and over a hundred articles and book reviews in psychology or his hobby field of magic. His Jungian-oriented books include *Beginner's Guide to Jungian Psychology*, *Beginner's Guide to Revelation*, *Jungian Archetypes*, and *Your Shadow*.